Patricia Furness-Smith MA, BA (Hons), PGCE, FNCS, FIfL, FCIEA, MBACP, MBAPCA, JP is a psychologist and psychotherapist with over 20 years of experience, and a former air stewardess during her gap year while studying law. She has lectured in psychology, psychotherapy and psychopathology as well as teacher training for a number of institutions. Her main specialisms are phobias, particularly those to do with travel (aeroplanes, boats, trains, tube trains, cars, etc.) and couples therapy. Patricia has worked as a consultant with the Flying with Confidence course for over 10 years, helping thousands of people to reclaim or gain the ability to fly.

Captain Steve Allright BEng (Hons), CEng, MRAeS is a British Airways training captain on the Boeing 747-400 and has been a professional pilot since 1990. Having obtained his 'wings' from Oxford Air Training School, he joined the Boeing 757/767 fleet, flying as a First Officer around Europe, the Middle East and the USA. He was then selected to become a training co-pilot and licensed CAA examiner. He has been involved with the Flying with Confidence course for over 20 years and is now a director of the programme. He has clocked over 11,000 total flying hours.

The British Airways Flying with Confidence course is the original and market-leading UK course dealing with overcoming flying fears. It has been running for over 25 years and, since its inception, has helped more than 45,000 people overcome their flying phobias. They hold courses at five airports around the UK.

THE PROVEN PROGRAMME TO FIX YOUR FLYING FEARS

Patricia Furness-Smith and
Captain Steve Allright

Vermilion
LONDON

Published in 2013 by Vermilion, an imprint of Ebury Publishing
Ebury Publishing is a Random House Group company

The Random House Group Limited Reg. No. 954009
Addresses for companies within the Random House Group can be found at
www.randomhouse.co.uk

A CIP catalogue record for this book is available from the British Library

Penguin Random House is committed to a sustainable future for
our business, our readers and our planet. This book is made from
Forest Stewardship Council® certified paper.

Printed and bound in Great Britain by Clays Ltd, Elcograf S.p.A.

ISBN 9780091947859

Copies are available at special rates for bulk orders. Contact the sales
development team on 020 7840 8487 for more information.

To buy books by your favourite authors and register for offers, visit
www.randomhouse.co.uk

The information in this book has been compiled by way of general guidance in
relation to the specific subjects addressed, but is not a substitute and not to be
relied on for medical, healthcare, pharmaceutical or other professional advice on
specific circumstances and in specific locations. So far as the author is aware, the
information given is correct and up to date as at October 2012. Practice, laws
and regulations all change, and the reader should obtain up-to-date professional
advice on any such issues. The author and publishers disclaim, as far as the law
allows, any liability arising directly or indirectly from the use, or misuse, of the
information contained in this book.

The names and identifying features of people in the case studies have been
changed to protect their privacy.

Patricia and Steve dedicate this book to all course participants and clients, whose courage in confronting their fears has been inspirational.

We would also like to dedicate it to our colleagues in the British Airways Flying with Confidence team. Their professionalism, enthusiasm and commitment are what make the course such a resounding success.

Contents

Never surrender to fear as it
will steal your life

INTRODUCTION

A journey of a thousand miles begins with a single step.

Lao-Tzu

First of all, congratulations! You have started the process of tackling your fear of flying, a challenging process that takes a great deal of courage. Acknowledging that you experience difficulty, or even terror, in taking a flight is a very positive sign, and picking up this book shows that you intend to do something about it. Well done. This, in itself, is a huge step forward towards defeating the problem.

Sadly, many people don't even get this far. Some remain in denial and try to pretend to themselves that they can get by perfectly well in life without ever needing to fly. Others, who resign themselves to the fact that they have no choice and *must* fly on occasions, allow their fear of air travel to become progressively worse. They choose not to address the cause of the problem but mask the symptoms by increasing the amounts of drugs and alcohol they take to help them get through the flight.

By choosing this book you have shown your desire to change and your intention to challenge your fear constructively. Here we will give you the knowledge of a pilot and the skills of a psychologist; and these resources will give you what you need to face your fears and take back control of your life.

Don't be Restricted by Your Fears

Roughly one in three people are affected by a fear of flying, which ranges from mild discomfort to severe terror. Fear of flying can include these symptoms: feeling out of control, panic attacks, claustrophobia, security concerns, the fear of crashing and many others.

Such feelings can strike anyone, no matter what their age, and can have far-reaching effects on many areas of life. Overcoming your fear of flying could mean accepting an exciting career promotion elsewhere, attending an important family wedding, enjoying a fabulous holiday abroad or receiving important medical treatment. On the other hand, ruling out air travel because of your fears will inevitably restrict what you do and what you can achieve.

Trust the Experts

This is where we come in. We are Captain Steve Allright, a highly experienced BA pilot and training captain on the Boeing 747-400 with over 20 years' flying experience, and Patricia Furness-Smith, a psychologist and psychotherapist who specialises in phobias, particularly to do with travel. Together we work on the British Airways Flying with Confidence course, a programme that was set up to help nervous flyers overcome their fears and has, so far, managed to help over 45,000 people do just that.

On the course, we each use our own area of specialist knowledge to deal with the two main aspects of a fear of flying. These are a lack of understanding about how flight happens, and the onset of panic and anxiety symptoms caused by flying and how to deal with them.

The course begins with a presentation from a BA pilot, such as Steve, who explains the technical aspects of flying and provides the knowledge that will help put your mind at rest. This is followed by a presentation from a psychologist, such as Patricia, who explains exactly what is happening when you suffer with irrational fears and how to deal with them. The aim is to provide you with all the information you need and the coping strategies to manage your anxiety to enable you to defeat your phobia entirely or, at the very least, learn how to manage it more comfortably so it doesn't rule your life. The grand finale of the one-day course is when the participants put their newly acquired skills into action by taking a short flight with a running commentary on all the noises and sensations. For all participants it is a liberating and life-changing experience.

However, most of us lead very busy lives, and not everyone has the resources or the time to take part in the Flying with Confidence course. We've recognised the need for a helpful guide that you can refer to again and again, or show to your friends and family who may need help to understand your fear of flying, why it is so debilitating for you, and the measures you're undertaking to overcome it. What we have done in these pages is to take and expand on the material we cover in the programme and give you a clear plan of action on how to conquer your phobia.

As in the course, Steve clearly explains the mechanics of flying and helps to put to rest some of the worries you may have about flight, including turbulence, that dropping sensation as the aircraft lifts off the runway, and simple ways to make your flight more enjoyable, while Patricia looks at the psychology of fear of flying and gives you the psychological tools to defeat it. Whether your phobia is paralysing and feels insurmountable, or you are just getting more and more edgy each time you fly, the principles for overcoming your fears are the same.

How to Navigate this Book

As we have mentioned, a fear of flying is commonly based on two things: a lack of knowledge about how an aeroplane actually operates and irrational fears that cannot be explained. Therefore, we have divided the book into two main sections and use our individual areas of expertise to deal with each of these respectively. Obviously, both sections are important but if, for example, you are much more worried about how to control a panic attack when it does strike than how an aircraft actually manages to stay up in the air, then it's a good idea to read the psychological section first. This is important because once you feel confident about the most frightening aspect of your phobia you will feel more relaxed and better able to absorb the rest of the material in the book.

Part one: the technical side of flying

Part One deals with the key technical aspects of flying. Understanding the principles and technology of how the aircraft gets up in the air and stays there will provide you with the knowledge you need to help you feel confident that flying is the safest form of travel. In this section, you will also learn the basic principles of flight, including how the aircraft operates, how much training a pilot undergoes, how the weather affects wind conditions and most importantly that turbulence is a totally natural part of flying and is never dangerous!

Part two: the psychological tools for mastering your fears

Part Two looks at the psychological issues that affect you if you have a fear of flying. These are largely to do with a

4

feeling of a loss of control and fear of having a panic attack, along with specific difficulties relating to claustrophobia, acrophobia, agoraphobia, emetophobia and social phobias. It also, most importantly, gives you a 'psychological toolbox' – a range of highly successful tried-and-tested techniques that you can call upon at any time, to defeat your fear and stay in control of what is happening. The good news is that, once these coping strategies are in place, you will have the confidence in knowing that there is no situation that you cannot deal with. In fact, the techniques outlined in Part Two will give you a range of transferable skills to help you to deal with fear, panic and anxiety in any situation, be it sitting an examination, addressing a conference or meeting your future parents-in-law for the first time. Knowing that you can rely on such coping strategies will give you the confidence to handle anything that life throws at you.

> *Your life doesn't get better by chance, it gets better by change.*
>
> Jim Rohn

Be open to new experiences and learning new things. It is very important that you do not limit your ability to change. Whether you have had a problem with flying for many years or it has just started recently, you will get much more out of this book if you approach it with curiosity, rather than thinking that you had tried to overcome your fear before and nothing has worked. By opening your mind and trusting in the process, you will be more likely to overcome your phobia and be able to fly with confidence. Remember: 45,000 people have come through our course successfully. You can too.

PART ONE

THE TECHNICAL SIDE OF FLYING

Captain Steve Allright:
BA Pilot and Training Captain

For most people, whether they experience a fear of flying or not, everything, from that first 'bing bong' as the 'fasten seatbelt' sign comes on until the aeroplane finally reaches a standstill after landing, is unknown to them. And for people who do have a fear of flying, that lack of knowledge can be debilitating. They often interpret the normal sounds of flight as something more sinister, but find that once they understand where the noises come from and their part in the flight, their minds are put at rest. Therefore, my aim in this section is to dispel all those myths and preconceived ideas you've gathered over the years about flying.

In over 20 years as a BA Pilot, I've learnt that the common factors that lead to a fear of flying are a lack of control, a lack of knowledge and a lack of familiarity. As the saying goes, with information comes power, and learning about the technical side of flight will help you understand how an aeroplane gets up in the air and stays there until it reaches its destination and the pilot is able to bring it in to land. I have found that with an understanding of the mechanics of flight, people feel more in control, and calmer.

I will also outline the lengthy and comprehensive training process that people have to go through in order to become a pilot on a commercial aircraft; while you may not be in control while on a flight, you can be reassured that the aeroplane is safe in the hand of professionals. I will then give you the knowledge about what happens when the aircraft takes off and lands. It's important to know just what causes those unusual sensations, such as that sinking feeling just after take-off that we all experience when we fly, and what is meant by turbulence and why it is a perfectly natural everyday occurrence. This should address the lack of familiarity that causes such concern and anxiety.

I hope you enjoy the technical section and remember: knowledge is power!

CHAPTER 1

THEORY OF FLIGHT

How an Aircraft Flies

I n this chapter, I will guide you through the basic principles of flight. Just how does all that metal get, and stay, airborne? The basic theory is, in fact, quite straightforward. Imagine a bird soaring through the sky, a bird of prey perhaps, or a seagull floating on the breeze. The key point here is that the bird is not flapping its wings to stay airborne, rather it is perfectly balancing the forces acting on it: lift, weight, thrust and drag.

As you stand on our planet, you are experiencing gravity, giving you *weight*. As you start to walk along, or even run, you are using your muscles to create *thrust*, and immediately this is countered by *drag*, the wind that you feel against your face. The only force you are not experiencing is lift. However, if you were to suddenly strap yourself into a hang glider, you do not have to run very fast to experience the force of *lift* as well.

Therefore, anything that incorporates a wing or other lift-producing device has four forces acting upon it (see the image below). As soon as any animal or flying machine creates more lift than its own weight using airflow over its wings, it will go up, and will stay up if the lift is in balance with the weight. The only other two forces that need to be balanced are thrust and drag. All four forces are explained within this chapter.

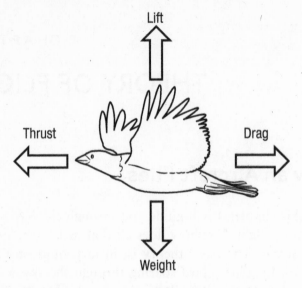

The forces acting on a lift-producing device.

Lift

How is it that 400 metric tonnes of aircraft, fuel, passengers and cargo can lift smoothly into the air? And how does it stay up there, hour after hour, with seemingly nothing below it? The answer is *lift*. Lift from the wings. As long as the aircraft is going forward, the wings are producing lift. Even when the aircraft is descending, the wings are producing lift. In fact, when it is time to descend, we reduce the engine power back to idle, and the wings continue to provide enough lift to glide the aircraft completely safely until we need to level off or stabilise the aircraft on the approach, at which time we increase engine power once again. Commercial aircraft can glide approximately 100 miles (160 km) from cruising altitude with no power from the engines at all.

WHAT IS LIFT?

So what is lift? How is it produced? To answer these questions properly we must first grasp the concept of air having fluid properties. Think of the air all around us as an ocean, having the same properties as the sea, other than the fact you can't see it!

For proof that something is there, next time you are a passenger in a car, put your hand out of the window. Holding it palm down you'll feel virtually no resistance, but turn the palm towards the on-rushing air and you'll feel quite a lot of resistance at high speed. Imagine a small piece of metal doing the same thing, and now a bigger piece of metal, and think about all the resistance that would cause.

You are now ready for the theory of lift, which was named Bernoulli's theorem, after its formulator Swiss physicist Matthew Bernoulli. Take a look at the image below. The shaded aerofoil is a cross section of a wing and, as the aircraft is propelled forwards, the wing slices through the air, forcing some air over the top of the wing and some underneath.

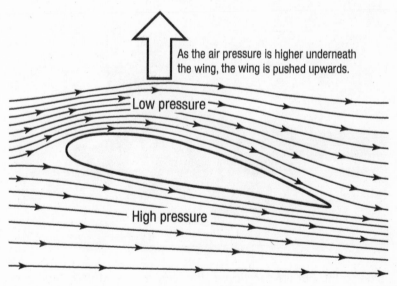

As the air pressure is higher underneath the wing, the wing is pushed upwards.

Low pressure →

High pressure

Bernoulli's theorem.

Crucially, the shape of the wing and the slight 'angle of attack', also shown, causes the air moving over the top of the wing to travel further and therefore faster to reach the point at the back of the wing than the air underneath. Forcing the air to move faster over the top of the wing causes low pressure, or suction, above the wing and relatively high pressure below the wing. The resultant force is lift.

The following photograph shows a 747 approaching to land in very humid conditions. When the weather is fine, it is impossible to see lift, or more specifically the huge suction that is created by the shape of an aircraft wing. But on humid days, like the day this photograph was taken, it is possible to see it with the naked eye. The low pressure caused by the shape of the wing causes a 'cloud' to form above the wing, which effectively reveals the suction, or lift, that makes an aircraft fly.

Due to the humid conditions, the 'cloud' of suction is revealed over the wings on this aeroplane as it comes in to land.

CAN YOU PROVE IT?

The theory behind lift is based on the law of physics that states that air separating above and below a surface must reach the same point, whichever route they take. If the air above the surface moves faster than the air below, it creates low pressure. To prove to yourself that this theory works, try this simple experiment.

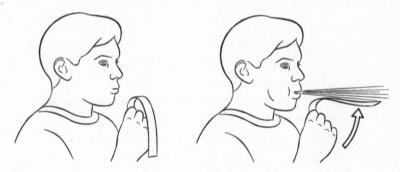

Demonstrating the principles of Bernoulli's lift.

1. Take a thin strip of paper and hold it by one end.
2. Place your mouth very close to the end of the paper you are holding, just above the top surface of the paper.
3. Blow gently across the top of the paper, thereby simulating the faster moving air over the top of a wing. The paper will rise due to the reduction in pressure.

In the case of an aeroplane, it is simply a matter of manufacturing a wing big enough and moving it forwards fast enough to generate enough lift to support the weight of the aircraft and all its contents.

It is the wings that enable the aircraft to fly, not the engines.

HOW THE PILOT USES WING FLAPS

It goes without saying that the lift must exactly match the weight of the aircraft in flight in order for it to fly straight and level. The wing is designed to be an appropriate size to do this at cruising speeds of around 500 mph (805 kmph). But what about take-off and landing? Safety would be compromised to take off or land at that sort of speed and you would need a very long runway to do it. So, instead, we temporarily increase the size of the wing by extending the flaps (on the back of the wing) and slats (on the front). Take a look at the images below and opposite to see what they look like. The pilots will generally extend the flaps just after they have started the engines and just before they taxi. If you are sitting approximately halfway down the aircraft, you may even hear the hydraulic jacks whirring as the flaps are extended. Next time you hear this noise, you can relax in the comfort of knowing that this is perfectly normal and understand why it is happening.

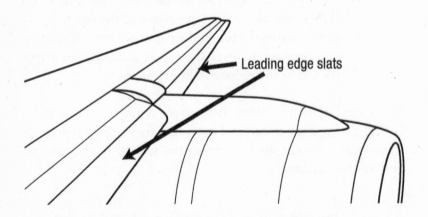

Leading edge slats

The slats on the front of the wing.

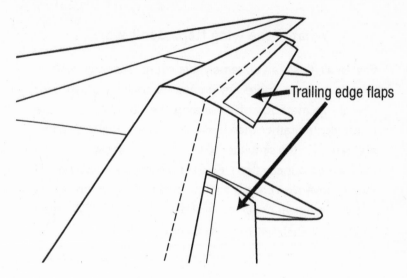

Trailing edge flaps

The flaps on the back of the wing.

After take-off, the flaps and slats are then retracted in stages as the aircraft accelerates, creating more lift, which requires a smaller wing. When preparing to land, the flaps and slats are extended once again to make the wing bigger and enable the aircraft to land at reasonable speeds.

Each time the flaps on the wing move there will be noises and sometimes vibration in the cabin; this is perfectly normal.

What if the wing flaps don't work?

First of all, this is an extremely rare event. Secondly, with all aircraft systems, there are numerous back-up systems or alternative methods of extending the flaps, for example using electric rather than hydraulic power. Finally, all pilots are trained in the simulator to land the aircraft safely at high speeds without any flaps. Flapless landings are also part of every conversion course a pilot undertakes and forms part of the three-year check cycle laid out by the Civil Aviation Authority (CAA) that all pilots have to undergo.

Weight

I have already talked about the need to balance lift and weight, but how do we actually know how much an aircraft weighs? There are five things that make up the weight of an aircraft, so let's look at each of these in turn.

1. **Basic weight of the aircraft**. Do we know how much the aircraft weighs? Well actually, yes, every aircraft is weighed as it leaves the factory on a giant weigh bridge. When new paint is applied, this is weighed also, and can be several metric tonnes!
2. **Fuel**. When the flight crew decide how much fuel they need to have loaded on board, the fuel order is actually placed by weight. Not by gallons or litres, but by metric tonnes. The actual fuel loaded is carefully checked so the exact weight is known.
3. **Passengers**. This is the only fraction of the total weight that is estimated. Naturally, the estimation is very conservative

and well educated, based on the breakdown of adult males and females, children and infants. This is also only a very small percentage of the overall weight of a loaded aircraft. In fact, when the take-off speeds are calculated, the assumption is made that all the passengers are adult males.

4. **Baggage**. All hold loaded baggage is weighed at check-in. A running total is kept and used for final take-off calculations.
5. **Cargo**. All hold loaded cargo is also very carefully weighed and checked.

I worry about how much hand luggage people bring on board

Don't! Consider a 747-400 jumbo jet on the way to Johannesburg, for example. The jumbo weighs about 400 metric tonnes when fully fuelled and full of passengers and cargo. But let's break that down into components to understand why you shouldn't worry about a few extra bags of duty free. Here are actual figures from a recent flight to Jo'burg. The basic weight of the aircraft alone is 190 tonnes and the fuel we will carry weighs 120 tonnes, so that's 310 tonnes. The weight of the cargo is 20 tonnes and the total weight of the 300 passengers and cabin baggage is estimated at just 30 tonnes. Average weights are used to estimate male, female, children and infants. So, out of a total of 360 tonnes total weight, less than 10 per cent is made up of passengers and cabin baggage. As there is a 10 per cent safety margin applied to all take-off speed calculations anyway, even if every one of the 300 passengers is a huge male who is carrying an oversized cabin bag, you will still be safe.

HOW DOES THE WEIGHT AFFECT TAKE-OFF?

The actual weight of the aircraft, fuel, cargo and luggage is known very accurately, with only the passengers estimated as explained previously. Other elements are also taken into consideration: wind, the ambient pressure and temperature, the runway length and height above sea level. All this information is carefully loaded into an on-board computer that produces our take-off speeds, which are then carefully checked.

WILL THERE ALWAYS BE ENOUGH FUEL?

Yes. The amount of fuel we carry is calculated using a very sophisticated computer model that constantly collects and updates real time wind and temperature information from aircraft flying around the world. This provides an incredibly accurate estimate of how much fuel we will use for the flight, and is known as our trip fuel. We then add our diversion fuel, just in case the weather is not suitable at our destination, or there is some other problem with the airfield that might cause us to divert, such as the runway being blocked. We add our taxi fuel, and on top of all that we carry a minimum reserve fuel, which gives us 30 minutes of flying time. Finally we add contingency fuel on top of everything for unforeseen circumstances.

The flight crew carefully review the weather at destination and along the route at the briefing stage, when the fuel decision is made. A gross error check of the fuel suggested by the computer model is made and all other factors are considered before a final fuel decision is made. The captain has the final say, and although we are encouraged to be commercial in our thinking, *British Airways flight crew are never put under duress to take minimum fuel.*

WHY AREN'T THE FUEL TANKS FILLED TO CAPACITY?

Fuel is very expensive, and weighs a lot, so for every 10 metric tonnes of extra fuel you carry on a 10-hour flight, you will burn three metric tonnes just to carry it. Flight crew are encouraged to carry the minimum safe fuel to save money and reduce pollution, but the operating crew always have the ability to carry extra fuel if they anticipate delays.

The only time we would take a lot more fuel than we actually need would be when the fuel is very expensive to buy at our destination, if there is a shortage or, occasionally, no fuel at the destination airfield. This is called tankering.

Thrust

We have seen previously that it is the wings that enable the aircraft to fly, not the engines, but in order to take off in the first place we have to create enough lift to get airborne. To create enough lift, we have to accelerate the aircraft to a speed at which the wings are producing the appropriate amount of lift. We then need to create more lift than is needed to climb and, when established in the cruise (the level section of the flight that fills the majority of the time on most flights), we then need to overcome the drag of the aircraft to sustain level flight. On almost all international commercial aircraft this is achieved using jet engines. Some domestic (within the same country) airlines use propeller driven aircraft known as turboprops, as they are much more fuel efficient on short flights. By the way, they are just as safe as jets! I will outline in a moment how engines produce thrust, but first let me reassure you about the safety checks all engines undergo on a day-to-day basis.

ENGINES AND MAINTENANCE

All aircraft engines are extremely reliable and incredibly well maintained. I often ask the people in the Flying with Confidence class how many of them looked at their car to check basics such as tyres and oil levels before they drove to the course. Sometimes the odd one or two puts their hands up, but generally no one does this. Before each and every flight, a pilot will always walk around his or her aircraft to carry out a visual inspection, whether it's a single prop two-seater or a jumbo jet.

In addition, an engineer carries out the same but slightly more detailed inspection and makes an entry into the aircraft maintenance log (or 'tech' log) to certify that a transit check or more detailed check has been made. The captain will carefully check and sign this log before every flight.

So before every single flight, one of the pilots and a licensed engineer makes a visual inspection of the aircraft. In addition, every day of the year, every aircraft has a 'daily' or 'transit' check, which is more detailed than just a visual inspection. Think of it as actually lifting up the bonnet of your car and checking the oil, water, hydraulics and electrics. All the warning systems on board are checked; tyre condition and pressure and some very clever fault diagnostic computers are checked.

In addition to these daily checks, the aircraft undergoes a series of more thorough checks that are carefully laid out by EU law. These maintenance schedules stipulate how often and how in depth each check is. These are called A, B and C checks and are carried out based on the amount of flying the aircraft has done. The most rigorous of these checks will involve taking the aircraft into an engineering hangar for several weeks because the check is so thorough.

HOW DO ENGINES PRODUCE THRUST?

Suck, squeeze, bang, blow. As simple as that, really. The engines suck the air in at the front, squeeze the air through a series of rotor blades into a combustion chamber where aviation fuel is added and ignited – the bang – and the air is blown out of the back of the engine faster than it came in at the front. Sir Isaac Newton said for every action there is an equal and opposite reaction. Therefore, if the air is coming out of the back of the engine faster than it came in, the resulting force must be that the engine moves forward. As it is attached to the aircraft, the aircraft moves forward.

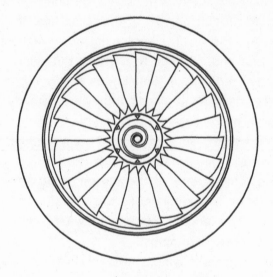

It is the engines on the jet that produce the power to provide the thrust.

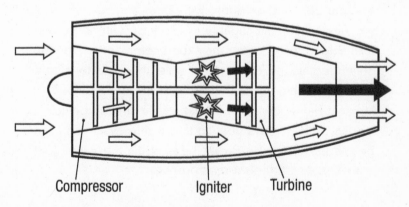

Compressor   Igniter   Turbine

Cross section of a jet engine.

What about the problem of birds flying into an engine?

Every new aircraft type is tested by firing an already dead bird, about the size of a chicken, into a running engine on a test rig. The engine must survive the impact of the bird and continue to produce thrust in order to pass initial certification. Small birds do occasionally get sucked into aircraft engines but they are instantly vaporised, with no damage to the aeroplane. Very rarely, a large bird enters an engine, or the aircraft flies into a large flock of birds, both of which can result in engine damage. This is one of the reasons that commercial aircraft have two engines, as the aircraft can fly very safely on one engine, something we practise in the simulator every six months.

In my 22 years of flying, I have only heard of one occasion when birds affected both engines. In January 2009 a US Airways Airbus had just taken off from LaGuardia airport in New York when it encountered a flock of Canada geese. Even then, with both engines affected, the wings were still capable of producing lift and therefore able to glide. Under the expert command of Captain Sullenberger, the aircraft was able to come to a safe landing on the Hudson River, with no loss of life. This incident highlights the fact that jet aircraft can be safely landed on water and float so that a safe evacuation can be made. Remember: *after take-off it's the wings that make an aircraft fly, not the engines.*

When British inventor Sir Frank Whittle first discovered the thrust capable of being produced by a jet engine, he had no idea how powerful and efficient engines would become. Modern commercial aircraft jets produce up to 100,000 lbs of thrust.

Drag

WHAT IS DRAG?

Drag is a force that is very easy to explain. Imagine that you are in car and you put your hand out of the window and face your palm against the airflow. The force you feel on your hand is drag. If you then hold your hand flat, palm down, the drag force is considerably reduced. It is the reason why supersonic aircraft have a sharp pointed and sleek design to create as little drag as possible, enabling these aircraft to break through the sound barrier, which, incidentally, provides drag of its own.

HOW IS DRAG RELEVANT TO AIRCRAFT?

When an aircraft (or any vehicle) is going forward, it constantly creates drag. The faster it goes, the more drag it creates. The drag of the aircraft has to be overcome on take-off by the thrust from the engines in order to create enough lift from the wings to fly. In the cruise, in order to maintain a steady speed, the engines must provide enough thrust to counter the drag being produced by the aircraft moving through the air. So in this sense you could say drag is a negative force, but we also use and vary the amount of drag produced by the aircraft during descent, approach and landing, and occasionally during the cruise.

Anything protruding from the smooth skin of the aircraft that can interrupt the smooth flow of air over the aircraft when the aeroplane is in flight creates extra drag.

The most obvious example of this is the undercarriage or, to use the American term, the landing gear: the structure that supports the aircraft on the ground. The landing gear creates quite a considerable amount of drag so is retracted very soon after take-off to help the aircraft accelerate; in the approach to landing it's usually lowered fairly late to reduce the extra fuel consumption that is caused by the increase in engine power required to stabilise the approach.

One of the more challenging aspects of being a pilot is ensuring that the descent and approach is flown at the correct height, which ensures the approach path is not too steep. This is primarily achieved by commencing the descent at the correct time but if it becomes clear that the aircraft is

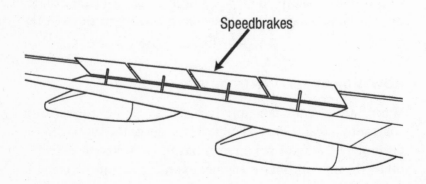

Speedbrakes

The most common way to increase the drag is by extending the speedbrakes or spoilers.

above the ideal approach path, the flight crew can increase the amount of drag created by the aircraft.

The most common way of increasing drag is to extend the speedbrakes (also called spoilers), see the image opposite. These are metal panels, usually on top of the wing (but on a few aircraft at the rear of the fuselage, the central body of the aircraft), which can be deployed using a lever from the flight deck. The amount of drag created by the pilot can then be varied by how much the panels are raised.

What causes that rumbling sensation and makes you feel like you are dropping?

The disruption in airflow when the speedbrakes are extended causes a light rumbling sensation in the cabin and you may feel the aircraft drop very slightly as the rate of descent is increased as a result of the extra drag. This is perfectly normal and an excellent example of how understanding something takes the fear out of what is otherwise an unusual sensation.

Very rarely, even the speedbrakes do not offer enough drag in order to increase the descent rate to the required level and, in these circumstances, the flight crew may decide to lower the undercarriage early. This creates a large amount of drag, especially at high speeds, and will also create a significant amount of noise and vibration in the cabin, which you will experience. Unusual, but all perfectly safe.

What would otherwise be an unexpected and potentially worrying event, can now be rationally explained and, better still, is probably the result of a runway change requiring an increased rate of descent, which means that you will be landing sooner than you thought!

In summary

One of the most important pieces of knowledge to help allay your fears about flying is to actually understand the theory of flight and how an aircraft stays up in the air. The key points to remember are:

- Bernoulli's theorem – the theory of lift. How an aircraft gets airborne, stays airborne and can even glide if the engines stop.
- The shape and size of the wing can be changed by slats and flaps to produce more lift for take-off and landing. When these are moving, they make a strange sound but are all part of the normal flight process.
- The required fuel for any flight is always very accurately calculated and there is a huge amount of extra fuel carried to cover any eventuality. The flight crew always have the last say on how much fuel is carried.
- Commercial aircraft are incredibly well maintained and, as a result, are extremely reliable.
- The drag of an aircraft is the resistance it creates as it moves through the air. As well as moving the flaps on the wings, the pilots are also able to vary the drag of the aircraft using the speedbrakes or the undercarriage. This will always create some vibration in the cabin but is perfectly normal.

CHAPTER 2

PILOT TRAINING

Pilots are Highly Qualified Professionals

When you step on to an aeroplane, one of the most important things to remember is that you are in safe hands. The pilot and co-pilot sitting in the flight deck are highly trained, qualified professionals who have been put through the most rigorous and exhaustive training procedures that are intended to prepare them for almost any eventuality they may ever encounter in their flying career. In fact, this regime of comprehensive training and testing continues throughout their career in order to maintain the highest possible standards. It is important to remember, their number one priority is, and always will be, your safety and well-being.

It is perhaps worth pointing out here the irony of the fact that many of us will happily jump into a taxi, blissfully oblivious about the credentials of the driver, and yet are extremely nervous of showing that level of trust to the pilot of an aircraft who has trained long and hard and whose competency is rigorously challenged throughout their career with constant checking procedures.

For pilots working for British Airways, every six months we surrender our flying licence to a training captain or training co-pilot for two days of intensive testing and training in order to be allowed to continue flying. This is true of all airlines that fly into or out of the UK, as they will all fall under the law of the European Aviation Safety Agency (EASA), the European civil aviation body that stipulates how often pilots must be checked.

At BA, like the majority of other airlines, we undergo an annual medical, two annual technical exams, and are continually improving our teamwork and non-technical skills, as well as our aircraft handling skills.

To illustrate this point and, I hope, reassure you further about the high standards a pilot has to meet, I think it is worth going into more detail about the depth of training a pilot has to undertake in order to be able to fly a commercial aircraft.

How hard is it to become a pilot?

The year I was selected for a sponsored BA cadetship, there were 12,000 applications for 200 places. Candidates were whittled down, firstly through the 11-page application form, and then by using a series of mathematical and verbal reasoning written exercises and a hand–eye coordination challenge. If you survived all of these you then had one final day of interviews and a group exercise.

A more recent example of pilot selection includes a check of previous education, work experience and the reasons for wanting to become an airline pilot, along with other criteria. If this initial screening is passed, then the selection progresses to group exercises, which assess whether you can work in a team, how you would deal with difficult situations and if you show command potential.

A form of aptitude testing has to be undertaken along with a mathematics test. The aptitude test consists of situational awareness, hand–eye coordination, the mental agility required to cope with multi-tasking, and the mental capacity to understand all the necessary skills it takes to become a pilot. The tests vary but one of the more difficult selection tests involves multi-tasking while scanning shapes and numbers, a crucial attribute for a pilot.

How difficult is training?

All pilots have to obtain a commercial pilot's licence to be able to fly commercial aircraft. The route to obtaining this may not be the longest when compared to other professions if tackled full-time, but it is, arguably, the most intensive, combining the study and dedication to prepare for and pass up to 14 ATPL (Airline Transport Pilot's Licence) exams, with a minimum of 200 flying hours. This includes basic flying skills through a series of progress tests, leading to the dreaded 'Instrument Rating' flying exam, still the most mentally demanding hour of my entire life.

What do pilots learn at flying college?

If you pass the pilot selection and you are offered a place on a full-time integrated course, the first step is to cover the theory required to gain the Airline Transport Pilot's Licence. This consists of 14 exam subjects ranging from the principles of flight and aerodynamics, to meteorology and general navigation. The training is very intense with full days in the classroom being taught by instructors and hours of further computer-based training, private study and practice questions. This stage typically takes five to six months. Some people liken this volume of content with the material read in a three-year degree.

If all of the exams are passed then the practical phase can begin. The cadet pilot starts basic training with a single engine aircraft, flying visually, by looking out of the window and using the natural horizon, and learning all of the basic skills required to fly an aircraft. During this period, the cadet pilot will gain many hours of flying the aircraft solo with nobody else on board, including navigation flights that they have never flown before. The cadet will build hours upon hours of practising landings and take-offs, and develop decision-making skills and general handling skills (steep turns, engine failures, forced landings, flapless landings, glide approaches, etc.). These skills make the pilot well prepared to deal with any unusual occurrences, such as a failure of the flaps or a failure of the engine that requires the pilot to land the aircraft safely in a field.

On completion of the single engine stage, the pilot will then move on to multi-engine aircraft, which may have a 'glass cockpit', where there are computer screens showing the pilot the same information found on conventional instrumentation. This prepares the pilot for an airline environment where many of the aircraft also have glass cockpits.

Many more techniques are taught in this phase of training, including asymmetric flight with one engine failed and instrument flying where the pilot has a panel placed over the window so he can use only the instruments to fly the aircraft (this training will also simulate failures of some of the instruments). There are also simulator details that have to be undertaken as part of this training. When this stage is completed and the pilot has undergone and passed a flight examination, a commercial pilot licence is awarded along with a multi-engine rating.

The pilot now moves on to the instrument rating, which is relying solely on instruments in a multi-engine aeroplane. When this rating is gained, the pilot will be able to operate within cloud in controlled airspace and fly the aircraft solely on instruments, while being able to deal with failures of the main instruments or engines and make precise departures and arrivals at airports using ground equipment placed at the airport.

How do new pilots make the transition from flying small propeller aircraft to jets?

The pilot next moves into a simulator to complete a multi crew cooperation certificate. The simulator is an exact replica of the flight deck of an airliner and is designed to handle just like the real aircraft. This stage is about working as a team effectively to solve problems quickly and efficiently (known as crew resource management) while also learning how to handle larger jet aircraft.

The pilot will now progress on to a type rating with their airline and, once again, go into a simulator only after passing more theory exams on the systems, displays, etc. This time the simulator is full motion, where it is designed to replicate every detail of the real aircraft and simulate what it feels like in real life. The simulators are so sophisticated and realistic that many pilots forget they are actually in a simulator after 'flying' for a couple of minutes. The pilot now learns how to handle the specific aircraft he will fly for the airline and learn exactly what to do with specific failures: engine failures and many different failures of systems and abnormal situations, which, although rare, have to be experienced and learnt.

Once complete, for pilots with no previous flying experience, a minimum of six take-offs and landings have to be completed in an aircraft carrying no passengers. A jet is taken out of service for a day just to complete this stage of training. After this, the pilot will have to complete line training under the supervision of a training captain and, after a set amount of time, finally become a fully qualified first officer, allowed to fly with normal line captains. From this point onwards, the pilot will gain the experience and expertise to become a captain and command an aircraft him- or herself. To gain the full ATPL licence, 1,500 hours must be logged fulfilling certain requirements. Many captains have 15,000-plus hours of flying experience.

Are pilots tested after they have qualified?

Having obtained your pilot's licence, you must revalidate it at least once a year for your entire career. At BA, this occurs in the form of a two-day simulator check every six months. During these two days, your licence is on the line as you are assessed by a qualified Civil Aviation Authority (CAA) examiner as to whether you are competent and it's safe to retain your licence. The check involves a rejected take-off, a flight during which an engine failure will occur very close to take-off and then using automatics and manual flying skills to land the aircraft safely. The first landing will be discontinued very close to the ground, forcing a 'go-around', still with an engine failed, followed by a safe landing after an approach, unassisted by our usual precision approach aid, the instrument landing system. While all this is going on, the flight crew must communicate and comply with air traffic control, keep the cabin crew and passengers informed and navigate the aircraft safely both vertically and laterally. Non-technical skills are also assessed.

Commercial pilots are the most regulated profession on the planet.

What situations are pilots trained for in a simulator?

Just about anything and everything you could possibly imagine. Engine failures, gear failure, flap failure, loss of electrics, hydraulics, volcanic ash encounter, decompression, fire, medical emergencies, stalling, rejected take-offs, non-precision approaches, pilot incapacitation, diversion. All of these things, and many more, are trained on an initial conversion course and then retrained on a rolling three-year cycle. Non-technical skills are also assessed and trained such as leadership, situational awareness, decision-making and teamwork.

Do pilots undergo any other tests or checks?

Every year, in addition to the simulator checks, each pilot has a medical and a technical exam and, at least every two years, undergoes safety equipment and procedure training and testing, and a line check on a normal flight with a training captain observing.

What sort of medical checks do pilots have?

Every year each pilot gets a thorough examination by an aero medical examiner (AME). Assisted by a trained nurse, some basics are covered initially such as eyesight, hearing, blood pressure, height and weight, haemoglobin level, urine and a heart echo cardiogram. The AME checks over the results of all these tests and then carries out a series of tests themselves, one to one, to assess as accurately as possible that the pilot is safe to hold the Class One medical certificate that is required by the CAA.

What if two pilots don't get along or disagree?

A major part of all training and testing revolves around what we in BA call non-technical skills (NOTECHS), which are broadly grouped into leadership, situational awareness, decision-making and teamwork. These skills are trained and assessed by the training captains and co-pilots who themselves have undergone training to do so. It has long since been recognised that less than optimum human factors can be a crucial part of any accident chain and, conversely, good NOTECHS can be pivotal in enhancing safety.

In summary

This brief explanation of the training that must be undertaken to become a pilot illustrates the depth of technical knowledge and skill that must be acquired and prepares a pilot for almost any eventuality in their flying careers.

Have faith in your pilots. I know many of you worry when you don't hear from them, especially when you think you should, such as when experiencing moderate turbulence. The reason that they don't speak to you at these times is because these situations are totally normal and the pilots consider them to be normal. Therefore, you can safely *assume that everything is normal unless you hear otherwise from the flight crew.* And when you do hear from them, you will hear a calm, reassuring voice because everything will be under control. It is always worth remembering:

- Training to be a pilot is extensive and highly regulated. All cadets must pass 14 different exams before they are allowed anywhere near any simulator controls.
- Extensive work is carried out in highly sophisticated simulators so that the pilot is equipped to deal with almost any situation they are likely to encounter while in charge of an aircraft and develop vital decision-making skills.
- A qualified pilot must revalidate his pilot's licence at least once a year for their entire career. This includes simulator exams, a thorough medical check-up and a comprehensive technical exam.

CHAPTER 3

HOW AN AIRCRAFT IS CONTROLLED

A ll modern jet aircraft are operated in the air using three main controls: elevators, ailerons and rudder. We also have a speedbrake, but this is not a primary flight control and is covered under drag (see Chapter 1, page 23).

Aircraft move in three axes: pitch, roll and yaw. The easiest way to understand this is to imagine yourself in a car. Pitch would be the feeling you get going up and down over a humpback bridge, roll would be what you feel on a road with a lot of camber that makes the car lean to one side and yaw is simply moving left or right horizontally. Each control surface affects each axis of movement.

Elevators and Pitch

The elevators are situated at the very rear of the aircraft, attached to the horizontal stabiliser, or tailplane (see image below). They are connected to the pilot's control column (Boeing) or side stick (Airbus) through a variety of electric cables and hydraulic actuators. Quite simply, when the pilots pull back on the stick, the elevators move up, producing a down force at the back of the aircraft which causes the nose to lift, increasing the pitch angle of the aircraft. This is exactly what happens on take-off.

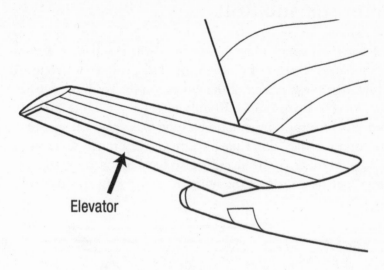

The elevators situated at the very rear of the aircraft.

This increase in pitch is what causes the sinking feeling you experience in your stomach just as you take off. The increase in pitch also causes an increase in gravity ('g' force). This is perfectly normal and will quickly pass as the aircraft establishes a steady pitch angle for climb out.

Sometimes I feel like I'm going over a humpback bridge. What causes that?

This feeling could be associated with turbulence, but more likely it is the exact opposite to what you are experiencing on take-off. By pushing forward on the control column, the elevators move down, raising the tail and dropping the nose. This is what happens at the start of any descent and may cause a slight weightless sensation, all perfectly normal.

Ailerons and Roll

Ailerons are small hinged sections on the end of the wing that control the roll of the aircraft. The primary ailerons are situated at the very end of the wings, on the trailing edge (see below). They are quite difficult to see on a large aircraft, and, because they are situated a long way from the centre of the aircraft, they don't have to move very much to create a rolling moment. Some aircraft also have inboard ailerons, or metal panels on top of the wing, to assist with roll control.

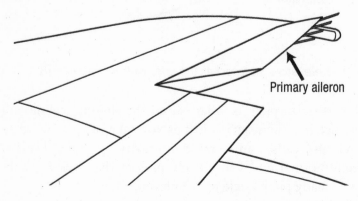

Primary aileron

The primary ailerons.

Unlike the elevators, which work in the same direction, the ailerons move in opposite directions. When a roll to the right is required, the pilots turn the control column (or move the side stick) to the right, the right aileron moves up and the left aileron moves down. By moving the right aileron up, a downforce on the end of the wing is produced, and at the same time, the lift at the end of the left wing is increased slightly by the aileron moving down, causing the wing to raise.

The combination of the ailerons moving in opposition causes the aircraft to roll, steering on to a new course as required.

Why do you have to roll at all?

If you have ever ridden a bicycle, you will have quickly learnt that in order not to fall off when going round a corner, you have to lean into the turn. This is exactly the same on an aircraft, except that you are travelling at much faster speeds. Huge centrifugal forces would make it feel extremely uncomfortable on an aircraft in a turn if the aircraft did not roll.

It feels like we are about to tip right over when the aircraft rolls. How likely is that to happen?

Although it is theoretically possible for the pilots to roll the aircraft as much as they want, it is extremely unlikely that you will ever experience any more than 30 degrees of bank. I know it feels like more than that looking out of the window, but this is a slight optical illusion. I can promise you that the pilots are monitoring every turn on their instruments, and the normal bank angle is just 25 degrees.

Rudder and Yaw

The rudder is attached to the back of the tail fin at the back of the aircraft, see image below. Almost every boat has a rudder, which sticks down into the water to help steer. Every aircraft has a rudder, which sticks up into the air to do the same.

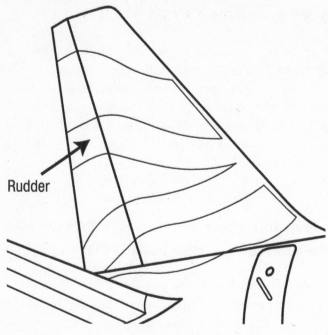

The rudder.

How do you steer on the ground?

When the aircraft is on the ground it is controlled by the tiller, a handle in the flight deck next to the pilots, which moves the nose wheel. The pilots can also control the nose wheel by moving the rudder pedals with their feet. The rudder pedal doesn't move the nose wheel as much as the tiller, but it does move the rudder as well.

How do the pilots keep the aircraft straight on the runway during take-off?

During take-off, the pilots do not use the tiller, as it could move the nose wheel too sharply. Instead, the pilots use the rudder pedals, which at the start of the take-off run will be using the nose wheel but, as the aircraft accelerates and the rudder becomes more effective due to the airflow over it, the rudder becomes the primary control surface.

What if an engine fails during take-off?

On every take-off, the pilots always calculate the speed at which it is safer to take off, rather than stop. This speed is called V1. So, if it is safe to stop, the pilots would reject the take-off by closing the thrust levers, ensuring that the speed-brakes deploy, selecting reverse thrust on the engines and applying the brakes; this braking is done automatically above a certain speed by pre-arming the autobrakes.

If it is safer to continue the take-off, it will always be possible to continue the take-off and climb away safely on the remaining engines. The rudder is applied, either manually by the pilots or automatically on the very latest aircraft types, to counteract the yaw that is caused by having more thrust on one side than the other. This is something on which training is given at the very start of your conversion on to any new type of aircraft and then practised and tested every six months in the simulator.

The Flight Deck

Quite a lot of the 'buttons' that you see when you first enter a flight deck are simply circuit breakers, like a fuse in a plug. The switches on the overhead panel are organised into groups such as hydraulics, electrics and air conditioning. Most of the switches and buttons on the aisle stand are communication devices such as radios and satcom.

The 'TV' screens in front of the pilots contain an array of primary flight information including attitude, speed, heading and altitude. They also display a moving map, which is used for navigation. Some of the screens are used to monitor the engines, aircraft systems, wheels and doors.

The obvious 'hardware' in the flight deck includes the thrust levers, control column or side stick, landing gear and flap, and speedbrake lever. All of these are connected to the controls via a system of electric and hydraulic components. Finally, the seats that the pilots sit on are fairly complex, being extremely manoeuvrable backwards and forwards, up and down, lumbar and recline, so that the pilot can position the seat in exactly the right position to operate the controls and pilot the aircraft safely. The image below shows all of these.

The instruments and controls in the flight deck.

In summary

In this chapter, you have learnt how an aircraft is controlled in three axes: pitch, roll and yaw and what each control surface is called and what it is used for. Many of the sensations you feel when you are flying are perfectly normal even though they feel very strange. Significantly, you now know:

- Why you feel heavier at take-off and sometimes weightless as you level off, both caused by the elevators controlling the pitch.
- That although when you bank it feels like the aircraft is really turning steeply, it is, in fact, only about an angle of 25 degrees and never more than 30 degrees.

CHAPTER 4

TURBULENCE

Without doubt, the single most common factor among fearful flyers is turbulence. Often we ask our course participants, 'Who doesn't like turbulence?' The response is an almost 100 per cent show of hands.

Many different things may cause turbulence, but each and every one of them is known and understood by your pilots. Every day I go to work, I expect a small amount of turbulence, just as I'd expect the odd bump in the road on the drive to work. Remember: *turbulence is part of flying*, and it is not to be feared. Many people I know, including Patricia, actually enjoy turbulence as it rocks them gently off to sleep. Babies especially, who know no irrational fear, are routinely comforted by what is, at the end of the day, part of nature.

In fact, out of all the many and varied causes of aircraft accidents, turbulence rarely, if ever, forms part of the accident chain. To that end, we approach the subject head on, with a mantra that states:

Turbulence is uncomfortable but not dangerous.

As you read through the chapter, I would ask that you repeat the above phrase over and over again. Every time you feel a wave of fear as you confront your own feelings on this

44

subject, repeat the phrase, either inwardly or out loud and proud! Then, when you next fly and experience turbulence – one of the most normal (and totally safe) sensations of flying – you should automatically say and repeat the phrase, and believe it, because it's true!

The Physics of Turbulence

Air has fluid properties. What does that mean? It means that just because you can't see it, it doesn't mean it's not there! A boat stays afloat because it rests on a body of water; an aircraft flies because it rests on a body of air. Just as the medium of water is subject to change and, as a result of the elements, can transform a glassy calm surface into a rough sea, the medium of air responds in a similar fashion. If you stir up the air a little, the aircraft experiences turbulence, *but the air does not go away*: it is still underneath you, like a vast ocean, enabling the aircraft to provide the lift that effortlessly supports the weight of the aircraft. The aircraft is built to more than withstand any turbulence that it may encounter and this poses no threat to its structure.

One analogy that might be helpful is of a cork on a river, with an ant living inside the cork. The river might be flowing quickly, and the edges of the river might be a little turbulent, but despite the rough waters, the cork is structurally unaffected and the ant happily reaches its destination, albeit a little queasy!

Why are some flights smooth and others scary?

The most frequent questions we get asked include: what causes the air to be stirred up? Why is it that some flights are smooth for hours and others give you a theme-park ride experience? The simple answer to all is the weather. Different aspects of the weather cause different types of turbulence. The weather is a big topic and we will discuss other non-turbulence related aspects of weather in the next chapter.

What is CAT?

CAT is an abbreviation for Clear Air Turbulence – the most common form of turbulence you are likely to experience, and is totally normal. Go back to your school days and recall, if you can, the water cycle.

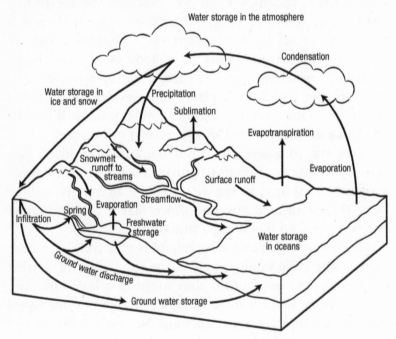

The water cycle.

In the water cycle, water is evaporated from the sea to form clouds. These drift over land and condense as rain, which falls from the clouds, then flows in rivers back to the sea again. The fundamental truth of this most basic of our planet's characteristics is that water is transported by moving large volumes of air up (carrying water as invisible vapour as it is evaporated), then as clouds (in which the water droplets become visible) and finally in a downpour as rain.

So, having proved that air can move around in a large volume, transfer that thought process to a global scale, where the Earth is rotating, and the huge land masses of our continents create air to rise and fall relative to the oceans. The net result is a continual flow of air around the Earth, which largely dictates our weather patterns. Visualise satellite images that you have seen on television of Earth from space depicting the movement of weather systems and air masses as they continually flow around our world.

The jetstream

The air tends to flow as a horizontal snaking river of air called a *jetstream*. A jetstream can sometimes be thousands of miles long but is usually only a few miles wide and deep. Depending on the direction of travel, our flight planners either avoid (into a headwind) or use (into a tailwind) these jetstreams to reduce fuel burn as they can flow up to 250 mph (400 kmph). The problem is, just like a fast-flowing river swirling against the riverbank, where the edge of the jetstream interacts with slower moving air, there can be some mixing of the air causing turbulence.

Forecasting turbulence

The problem is you cannot see CAT, you cannot detect it on radar and you cannot accurately forecast it. Sure, the meteorologists produce charts based on myriad computer analysis of continuously downloaded wind and temperature data from aircraft in flight to forecast areas of CAT. However, a bit like the British weather, the forecast at best is just that – a forecast, which is, even in these days of modern technology, an art rather than a science.

So, armed with these forecasts, we pilots do our best to warn the cabin crew (and sometimes the passengers as well) as to when it *might* be bumpy so that they can plan the meal service accordingly. In the main, however, we rely on reports from other aircraft, which we hear either directly or passed on by air traffic control. We then consider the options available to us. Our endeavours to fly at an altitude that has been reported as smooth may be prevented by several constraints such as other aircraft occupying that level or a higher level may not be possible due to the weight of the aircraft at that time. Jet engines are most efficient at higher altitudes and therefore the higher you fly, the less fuel you burn, so a move to a lower level will mean a reduced contingency fuel at destination.

Whatever the circumstances, you can rest assured that your pilot will find the most comfortable path to your destination without compromising your safety. Just like you, we experience the movement too and would prefer a smoother ride.

Uncomfortable but Safe

Flight crew around the world share a common classification of turbulence: light, moderate and severe. The definitions are laid down in our manuals and help us to make an assessment as to what our course of action should be. For the fearful flyer, even light turbulence can be upsetting. For pilots, light turbulence is no different to a bumpy road for a taxi driver or a slightly uneven section of track for a train driver – a small, but totally safe, inconvenience and very much part of our daily lives. It is a natural part of flying, and not to be feared.

Moderate turbulence

Moderate turbulence strikes no fear into pilots, as they will experience this level of turbulence for a few hours in every thousand hours they fly. It usually only lasts for 10 or 15 minutes, but rarely can last for several hours, on and off. This sort of turbulence will unsettle even some regular travellers and will cause drinks to slop and spill. No action is required by the pilot to control the aircraft, which is perfectly happy, but the flight crew may decide to try a different altitude if the turbulence persists. This is because they recognise that the meal service might be disrupted causing an inconvenience to hungry passengers.

Severe turbulence

Severe turbulence is *extremely* rare, although I meet people on every Flying with Confidence course who swear blind they have experienced it! In a flying career of over 10,000 hours, I have experienced severe turbulence for about five minutes in total. It is extremely *uncomfortable but not dangerous*. The aircraft may be deviating in altitude by up to 100 feet (30 metres) or so, up as well as down, but nothing like the thousands of feet you hear some people talking about when it comes to turbulence.

Air pockets are just a form of extreme mixing of air that may cause the aircraft to drop, just like a ship falling from the crest of a big wave to the natural level of the sea. Just like the ship, the aircraft will *not* continue to fall uncontrollably.

I should stress that this level of turbulence is so rare that leisure travellers will almost certainly never experience it and nor will most business people. The worst that can happen, and has happened, in these circumstances, is that passengers and crew that are not strapped in may injure themselves.

The aircraft is not in danger.

Aircraft designers are fully conversant with the worst that the elements can throw at them and modern airliners have been designed to withstand far in excess of the worst conditions that could ever be experienced. As part of the certification process that must be passed before production begins, any new airframe design is tested to destruction in a test rig.

Thunderstorms

Unlike CAT, pilots can see thunderstorms, either by the human eye by day, or by using weather radar by night (of which modern aircraft have at least two fitted for redundancy). Thunderstorms, or cumulonimbus, CBs in the trade, contain rapidly moving columns of rising and descending air, which can cause heavy rain, hail and lightning (accompanied by the sound of the electrical discharge – thunder).

Pilots like to avoid CBs (see page 60 for a diversion rating for thunderstorms). En route, we will take avoiding action sometimes hundreds of miles laterally to fly around them. If necessary, we will delay landing by holding or, if fuel reserves are low, diverting, to another airfield rather than land underneath or very close to a CB. By day, CBs are easy to spot, as they are very large, see upper image opposite. By night, we use a weather radar to detect CBs, see lower image 2 opposite.

Thunderstorms are clearly visible to the human eye by day.

Thunderstorms can be detected by weather radar at night.

Pilots would only ever consider flying in or close to a thunderstorm if *not* doing so would compromise the safety of the flight due to the proximity of other aircraft. The turbulence experienced inside the thunderstorm will be *uncomfortable but not dangerous*. There is an increased risk of a lightning strike, which all aircraft are specifically designed to tolerate. These strikes are actually quite common around the world and produce no adverse effect on the ability of the aircraft to fly safely.

Wind Effects

By this, we are talking about the effect of wind close to the ground as opposed to CAT, which occurs at cruising altitudes. If the Earth were truly a perfect sphere, with no hills, mountains, buildings, trees or even motorways, then theoretically wind effects close to the ground would not exist at all. The reality though is that the wind is affected by all those things. The mixing effects of the wind around tall buildings or nearby geographical features will increase as wind speed increases, causing low level turbulence. This sort of turbulence is generally light and lasts for only a few minutes after take-off and before landing. It's rarely uncomfortable and certainly not dangerous.

Windshear

Something that is regularly trained and discussed in the simulator is the cause, effect and recovery from windshear. This is the rapid change in the speed and/or direction of the prevailing wind close to the ground and is to be avoided during take-off and landing.

Windshear can be caused by weather fronts, CBs or just strong, gusty wind conditions and requires the flight crew to 'go-around' (discontinue the approach) until such time that conditions are safe. This procedure is practised in very realistic scenarios in the simulator during both initial and recurrent training, so that your pilots are always able to expertly handle such conditions.

Wake

Just like the wake of a speedboat or cruise ship on the ocean, so an aircraft leaves a trail of mixed-up air behind in its wake. For this reason, strict rules of separation between aircraft taking off and landing apply throughout the world. For example, a medium-size Boeing 737 will have to wait two minutes behind a Boeing 747 jumbo jet departing from the same runway to allow the air to settle.

Despite these precautions, flight crew do occasionally experience wake turbulence from another aircraft, usually when the wind is very light and exactly in line with the runway direction. Recovery from a gentle wing drop caused by this phenomenon is very straightforward and instinctive for the handling pilot.

In summary

Just occasionally, a ferry crosses the English Channel on water as flat as a mill pond, and so it is with flying that you may experience the odd, perfectly smooth flight. But it is more normal to experience a period of turbulence when you fly. Turbulence is one of the most normal and totally safe sensations of flying and is not to be feared. Having read this chapter, you might join me in a wry smile when I am warmly thanked by a disembarking passenger who says, 'Thank you so much for a nice smooth flight, captain.' As you now know, it has everything to do with nature and very little to do with me! It is important to remember:

- Turbulence is a stirring up of air.
- Turbulence is uncomfortable but not dangerous.
- Air pockets are just an extreme mixing of air that may cause the aircraft to drop, just like a ship on the crest of a wave. Just like the ship, the aircraft will not continue to fall uncontrollably.
- A pilot will find the most comfortable path to your destination without compromising your safety.

CHAPTER 5

WEATHER

n Chapter 4, turbulence is covered in depth, and some of the basics of meteorology (the weather) are discussed to explain what causes turbulence. In this chapter, I will explain every other aspect of the weather, from wind and rain to sun and snow, and everything in between.

Before I begin, I should emphasise that pilots are extremely weather aware. We have to study and pass exams in meteorology at Flying College in order to gain a flying licence. It forms a crucial part of every briefing before and during every flight, and because there is no aspect of the weather that is not understood, pilots take precautions to avoid situations in which they are exposed to the most severe weather. Pilots take great care never to expose themselves or their passengers to danger.

What is the Worst Type of Weather for Flying?

On our courses, I am often asked what is the most serious weather or the most dangerous for flight. Fog? Snow? Strong wind? In order to try to give some ranking, out of 10, as to what we would consider to be the most likely weather to cause us to divert, I have attempted to give a 'diversion rating' to each type of weather. The higher the number, the more fuel I would carry as I may have to divert.

These types of weather are not necessarily dangerous, and we pilots have been trained to deal with all kinds of conditions. I should emphasise that this is only my personal opinion, based on my flying experience to date and from listening to all the various diversion stories from my flying colleagues over the years.

> Severe weather should never cause you to be in danger; your pilots will avoid it.

Fog   DIVERSION RATING: 3/10

I have given fog a fairly high diversion rating, not because fog is particularly hazardous or difficult for pilots to operate in, but because it almost always results in delays. Almost every modern airfield has an Instrument Landing System (ILS) that enables aircraft to land safely in even the most limiting visibility. Some airfields, such as Heathrow, have an even more accurate system called MLS, which stands for Microwave Landing System. The reason for this is that the usual spacing applied between landing aircraft has to be increased in low visibility operations. This is because the ILS that we use to autoland in fog could be compromised by one aircraft landing just in front of another. The increased separation also gives plenty of time to vacate the runway before the next aircraft lands. Air traffic control call this the 'flow rate' and the result of a reduced flow rate almost always causes aircraft to 'hold' in a queuing system. So, if fog is forecast, or if the flight crew consider the conditions they observe in their briefing before take-off is likely to result in fog, many of us would consider extra fuel to enable us to hold for longer.

Hail   DIVERSION RATING: 1/10

Hail is normally only associated with thunderstorms or rapidly building clouds and therefore you would have to be flying inside such a cloud for the aircraft to be exposed to hail. While this is not impossible due to the constraints of crowded airspace, it is extremely rare and usually only occurs for a very short period of time. I have flown through hail a few times and, apart from being quite loud in the flight deck, it has absolutely no effect on the aircraft. I have seen photographs of aircraft that have been hail damaged by extremely large dense hail, all of which have continued to land safely.

Heavy rain   DIVERSION RATING: 1/10

It rains a lot in the UK but rarely heavy enough to cause us any concern. Modern aircraft engines can cope with a huge amount of water ingestion, such as flying through a dense rain cloud. The only real concern for pilots operating in heavy rain is a flooded runway. We refer to a very wet runway as 'contaminated'. In extreme cases, we would actually request the depth of contamination from Air Traffic Control, who have contact with airport operatives with equipment designed for just this purpose. Even then, because aircraft are very directionally stable on the ground and also equipped with extremely effective anti-skid brakes, it would take a huge and sudden downpour to render a runway unsuitable for take-off and landing.

High temperatures (and/or high altitude airfields) DIVERSION RATING: 0/10

When the air is very hot, it becomes very 'thin' and the engines don't run so efficiently and the wings don't produce as much lift, the same effect as being at a very high altitude, such as in Johannesburg (5,751 ft/1,753 m) or Mexico (7,350 ft/2,240 m). Sometimes we operate at airfields, which are both high altitude and also very warm. We call these airfields 'hot and high' and, although not dangerous, this combination presents a particular set of challenges to pilots. We just need a longer runway for take- off and landing and need to take into account how the conditions will affect the performance of the aircraft.

Ice DIVERSION RATING: 1/10

There are two effects of ice: one on the ground, and one in the air. In order to take off safely, the upper surface of the wing must be clear of ice. For this reason, aircraft are regularly de-iced first thing in the morning after a frost and before every take-off if icy conditions still exist. In the air, it is possible for ice to accumulate on the wings, usually on the leading edge, during flight through cloud when the air temperature is close to freezing. All commercial aircraft have some kind of anti-icing and/or de-icing system on board, usually hot air taken from the engine and piped along the front of the wing. An icy runway would not be impossible to land on and airports situated in very cold climates often have heated runways.

Lightning DIVERSION RATING: 2/10

Lightning strikes are rare but the aircraft is well designed to cope with such an event. In fact, the strike usually has *no effect whatsoever* on the serviceability of the aircraft. This is primarily because all aircraft are fitted with static wicks at the rear of the wing and tailplane. These are about the size of a long pencil, and are specifically designed to discharge any excess static electricity that the aircraft may accumulate. A lightning strike can be quite alarming, as they usually result in a loud bang, but rest assured that they will have little or no effect on the safety of the aircraft. An extremely rare event that is also possible, following a lightning strike, is for a lightning ball to pass down the aisle, again with no adverse effect to the aircraft.

Snow   DIVERSION RATING: 3/10

Snow causes no problem to aircraft in the air but can result in delays on the ground. For the same reason that ice has to be removed from the wing, the same applies to snow. Heated de-icing fluid is used to remove any snow that has settled on to the wing and de-icing fluid is then applied to create a 'holdover time', which prevents any further snow that is falling settling on the wing.

Our pilots will always also carry out a visual inspection just before take-off from inside the cabin to check the wing is still clear. If you are ever on board an aircraft that has been de-iced, you may notice that the fluid applied is green or orange. This is deliberate to indicate that it is still present. It may appear quite 'gloopy' and, again, this is normal. As lift is created during the take-off roll, the fluid will evaporate and be clear shortly after lift-off. Landing on a snow-covered runway is not normal but is possible as long as the snow has been compacted.

The main problem with snow is that parking stands can become limited, as aircraft waiting to be de-iced occupy stands that would otherwise be vacated. After a sudden heavy snowfall at a busy airport, it is possible to have to wait on the ground for a stand, or even be diverted to another airfield until parking space becomes available.

Strong winds   DIVERSION RATING: 4/10

Strong winds are caused by many different types of weather, and aircraft are well equipped to handle them. Each aircraft type has its own limit of course, typically around 70mph, or, if the wind happens to be across the runway, called a crosswind, nearer 50mph. Taking off or landing in a crosswind can appear to be quite dramatic from outside the aircraft, and can feel quite uncomfortable inside as well. Pilots are trained for this challenge, and we take professional satisfaction at handling it safely. Of course, if the wind is extremely gusty or outside of limits, the pilots will 'hold' to wait for the wind to subside or divert the aircraft, depending on how much fuel they have.

Thunderstorms   DIVERSION RATING: 5/10

Cumulonimbus cloud, or 'Charlie Bravos', CBs, as we call them (see previous chapter, page 50), present probably the biggest challenge to a planned arrival. Flight crew would be highly unlikely to take off or land with a huge thunderstorm overhead because of rapidly changing wind conditions, lightning and heavy precipitation in the form of rain or hail.

Fortunately, commercial aircraft are fitted with high technology weather radar that detects this precipitation, enabling the flight crew to identify a thunderstorm from over 100 miles (160 km) away and take avoiding action, day or night. It is possible to fly through a thunderstorm safely, and sometimes this is necessary because of crowded airspace. This will feel quite turbulent and uncomfortable in the cabin, but is totally safe. Thunderstorms are really only a problem if there is a big storm over an airfield you are trying to land at. The wind around and beneath a thunderstorm can change in speed and direction very quickly, which would change the amount of lift being produced by the wings.

However, flight crews will always try to avoid thunderstorms if possible, using weather radar and the help of Air Traffic Control.

In summary

I hope the chapter you have just read has reiterated the point that the majority of today's commercial aircraft are built to cope with almost all weather conditions, even in the extreme. Understanding how the different weather systems affect the air conditions – be it snow, ice, fog or heat – and therefore flying conditions will, I hope, help you appreciate how well an aircraft is equipped to fly in all weathers. It is important to remember:

- Pilots are extremely weather aware and it forms a crucial part of every briefing before and during every flight.
- They will take every precaution to avoid situations in which they are exposed to the most severe weather.

CHAPTER 6

AIR TRAFFIC CONTROL AND SECURITY

Air Traffic Control

Air traffic controllers are indeed the unsung heroes of aviation safety. They are selected for their skills of concentration, being able to think in three dimensions and, probably most of all, being able to stay calm under pressure. They are trained to a similar level as pilots and have to obtain an Air Traffic Control Licence (ATC) to be able to work. They are constantly checked and monitored, and because of the high level of intensity and stress that the job can entail at busy times, they work for short periods over a shift.

Do all air traffic controllers speak English?

Yes. Throughout the world, all pilots and air traffic controllers speak a common language, English. It is not unheard of to hear certain nationalities speaking their native tongue to their native pilots for short periods, but generally the rule is well observed.

Do pilots always operate in metric units?

Actually, we are mainly imperial. Probably two-thirds of the airspace we fly in is controlled in thousands of feet, or 'flight levels'. China and large parts of the former USSR operate in metric levels, which requires a slight altitude adjustment when entering into and leaving this airspace.

What if an air traffic controller makes a mistake?

This is a very rare event indeed but within the last 20 years the aviation industry has implemented technology that has made flying even more safe. Traffic Collision and Avoidance System, or TCAS as we call it, is a very clever piece of technology, which effectively allows aircraft to talk to each other and warn the pilots if the computer thinks that the normal safe protected area is about to be infringed. Have a look at the image below to see how other aircraft are presented to us in the flight deck on one of our cathode ray screens. If the TCAS equipment thinks our protective bubble (see image overleaf) will be infringed some

The screen in the flight deck showing other aircraft in the area.

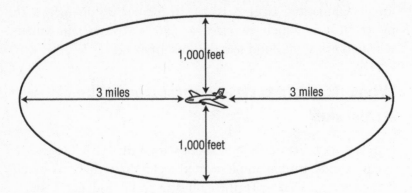

The protective bubble around the aircraft.

time in the next 60 seconds, a 'soft' aural warning sounds in the flight decks of each aircraft, initially to alert the pilots to a developing situation. Then a command will be issued in one flight deck, with the aircraft still miles apart, opposite to the one in the other flight deck, such as *'climb'* in one and *'descend'* in the other. As the pilots react fairly promptly, because plenty of notice is given, this is not a violent manoeuvre. In fact, the passengers may not even be aware that such a rare event is happening.

Security

For many, security is the number one concern when it comes to flying. I will attempt to reassure you in this short section that flying is as safe and secure as it possibly can be. I also hope that you will be reassured that I am severely limited in how much I can divulge in a publication such as this without compromising some of the training and procedures that we have in place. I can promise you that there is a whole lot more going on behind the scenes than contained within these short paragraphs.

I'm worried about terrorist activity. Do you think anything will happen?

I am very tempted to give a categorical 100 per cent '*no*', but that might be tempting fate. What I can tell you is that, as with any aircraft incident that involves loss of life, every time any terrorist activity affects aviation, there is a significant amount of new legislation. An example of this, since I started flying, is the protection of the flight deck and flight deck access. Electronic keypads and cameras are just a small but obvious part of the new technology and procedures that have been put in place over the years.

Are all airport staff security checked?

Yes. All airport staff, from pilots to cleaners, are security screened at the highest level and re-screened every few years when their security pass automatically expires. This involves a significant amount of official paperwork and photo ID. As well as entering 'airside', which is effectively the first security cordon, every cleaner, caterer, engineer or crew member has to show a security pass at the aircraft door to gain access to the actual aircraft. This task is carried out by security staff, who themselves have to be rigorously checked. The crew take over this task during boarding and on turnarounds where they are staying on board.

Do crew have to go through the same security checks that the passengers do every time they go to work?

Yes. Exactly the same set of rules apply. Our hand baggage is checked for liquids, gels and creams, just the same as passengers. We pass through a metal detector as used by passengers and we are subjected to random 'pat downs' or 'frisks', just the same as passengers.

What about hold baggage screening?

All hold baggage is screened according to the rules and regulations that apply.

I sometimes worry about certain individuals on board. What can I do?

If you have any concerns at all, tell the cabin crew. They are well trained in dealing with a scenario such as this and will know exactly what to do.

In summary

I hope that you are now reassured to know that as well as a crew of highly qualified pilots in charge of operating the aircraft, there is also a substantial technically trained team on the ground supporting their every move, providing instructions, advice and information as well as carrying out rigorous checks on anyone boarding that aircraft. They all have one aim: to ensure the flight's safety. To this end:

- Air Traffic Control are all trained to a similar level as pilots and are constantly checked and monitored.
- Security is top priority. All airport staff, from the pilots to the cleaners, are subject to the highest level of security checks.

CHAPTER 7

CIVIL AVIATION LAW AND EMERGENCIES

Take one look at a busy airport and most people would wonder how on earth (or not on earth!) accidents don't happen more regularly. One of the reasons that air travel is so safe is because anything and everything to do with aviation is regulated and governed by law. The actual pecking order of the National, European and International Law is quite complicated depending on which country you are operating from but, rest assured, the intention is always the same: *safe air travel.*

Aviation Law

What is covered by the law?

Everything from manufacture and certification of new aircraft through to maintenance schedules, pilot training, licensing and checking of flight crew, cabin crew, air traffic controllers and aircraft engineers, to the actual operating rules and air traffic control. Chief executive officers and chief pilots are responsible for maintaining an Air Operators Certificate, and each aircraft holds a Certificate of Airworthiness.

How does aviation law help prevent accidents?

Firstly, it gives airport authorities, airlines and air traffic control a set of rules to operate to. Secondly, it ensures that every aviation-related person that is involved in any potential accident chain has been properly selected, trained, tested and security checked. Finally, and specifically to pilots and cabin crew, emergency training is laid down and mandated.

Dealing with Emergencies

What sort of emergencies are flight crew trained to deal with?

In Chapter 2 (page 33), I listed some of the emergencies that we are trained to cope with. The important point here is that we are trained and regularly tested to be able to cope with *any* emergency that we may be faced with. On the Flying with Confidence course, we often get asked about all sorts of 'what if..?' scenarios. We always have an answer because anything and everything is trained for in the simulator.

How often do emergencies occur?

Incredibly infrequently compared to the huge amount of aircraft movements and flights around the world. Quite a lot of people who attend our courses feel that they have experienced an emergency landing but, when questioned further, very few have. Your perception of an event may be very different to reality. A good example of this is a 'go-around' (a landing that is 'discontinued' on its final approach). I often meet people who describe this event as an 'aborted landing', or other such colourful language. The reality is that a go-around is a very routine event for flight crew, and one that we brief and prepare for before every approach.

What causes an aircraft to go-around?

The most common cause of a go-around is at a busy airfield where the preceding landing aircraft is slow to clear the runway and therefore the safest course of action is to go-around. All other cases will be situations where the flight crew are not happy to continue the approach, possibly due to the weather conditions, or if the aircraft is not 'stable'. This is a point in space before landing at which the pilots must be satisfied that the aircraft is on the correct profile, all landing checks have been completed and the aircraft is at the correct speed.

IT FEELS VERY NOISY AND FRIGHTENING DURING A GO-AROUND. WHAT EXACTLY IS GOING ON?

I can relate entirely to the first half of this statement having experienced a go-around while seated at the rear of a 767 as a passenger. The sudden increase in engine noise, accompanied by a sinking feeling as the nose of the aircraft is raised and the rear of the aircraft initially goes down, is a really quite disconcerting experience.

The feeling in the flight deck couldn't be more different. The application of engine thrust is calmly applied, usually just by the press of one button, while simultaneously raising the nose either using the automatics or manually, and then some standard calls and actions are made, which include raising the flaps and gear, following the pre-assigned go-around route, and levelling off with the associated reduction in power. It is not always possible for pilots to explain ahead to passengers what is about to happen and they prioritise in the following order: aviate; navigate; communicate.

So what exactly is classed as an emergency?

Anything involving a fire would be considered an emergency and the initial call to air traffic control from the pilots would probably be a 'mayday' to indicate the safety of the aircraft is in jeopardy. The pilots would then carefully diagnose the problem and attempt to contain the fire. In the case of engines, all aircraft engines are fitted with fire suppressant, which can be activated from the flight deck. I recently read that there has *never* been an uncontainable fire on a Rolls-Royce RB211 engine, which is the one used on our 53 British Airways 747s and also on our 767 fleet.

This engine is typical of the type of jet used by *all* commercial airlines, for over 20 years, clocking up literally millions of hours. To have never suffered an uncontained engine fire in all those millions of hours is truly reassuring.

WHAT ABOUT A FIRE IN THE CABIN?

All our cabin crew and pilots are also trained in firefighting. This is done when you join and every year thereafter. The cabin crew also have a strict procedure in the unlikely event of any crew member discovering a fire on board. No matter how senior or junior, the first crew member to discover the fire becomes the 'firefighter', who calls for help to the next nearest crew member, who becomes the 'communicator', primarily to alert the flight crew to the danger and keep them appraised. The third and final part of the team becomes the 'coordinator', responsible for providing equipment to the firefighter and moving passengers as necessary.

The fire extinguishers on board commercial aircraft are like no other you can buy. They are green in colour and known as BCF fire extinguishers. Unlike conventional water or powder suppressants, these extinguishers put out fire by chemically reacting with the flame. They are *extremely* effective and would be used more but that they are not particularly environmentally friendly. Airlines have special dispensation to carry them because of the importance of extinguishing fire on board aircraft.

WHAT ABOUT ENGINE FAILURE?

Engine failure is probably the most rehearsed and prepared for event in the flight deck. It is our policy to run through each of our own actions in the event of engine failure on the first departure of every day. This way, in the unlikely event of it happening, our reactions would be almost automatic.

> All commercial aircraft can fly perfectly safely following the loss of an engine.

Engine failure is something we practise and are tested on in the simulator every six months. I myself have experienced a real engine failure on a 767 and I can assure you that the aircraft flies even more comfortably than the simulator!

WHAT IF SOMEONE IS TAKEN SERIOUSLY ILL ON BOARD?

This is undoubtedly our biggest cause for diversion. With the ever-increasing size of commercial aircraft, there is an increasing risk that someone will suffer an acute medical condition, such as cardiac arrest. Our cabin crew are medically trained and have a very comprehensive medical kit on board, including a defibrillator.

In the event of needing expert advice, we have two avenues that we can use. Firstly, an announcement may be made to ascertain whether a medically trained doctor is on board: the statistics of this being the case are incredibly high! Whether or not a doctor is able to assist, we also have access to a 24-hour medical helpline via the flight deck communication equipment, which enables us to speak to a doctor who will assess the condition by asking a series of questions. Often we would involve the cabin crew in that process.

In summary

When it comes to all aspects of flight, everything from the manufacture and certification of new aircraft, maintenance schedules, pilot training, licensing and checking of flight crew and operating rules are governed by strict laws and guidelines which are laid down to ensure maximum safety. This is very important when it comes to handling potential emergency situations as not only are the crew trained to the highest standards but there is also an exact protocol set down for them to follow to deal with all eventualities. It is also worth remembering that:

- Emergencies occur very infrequently considering the amount of aircraft movement around the world.
- The crew are trained and regularly tested to be able to cope with *any* emergency that they may be faced with.

CHAPTER 8

A TYPICAL FLIGHT

This chapter is written primarily with first-time flyers in mind, but it is also extremely useful for any nervous fliers to help them fully understand every aspect of the process. What follows is a brief explanation of everything you can expect on a typical flight, all the sights, sounds, sensations and things you might experience. Being armed with this knowledge, and knowing what to expect, will hopefully give you the confidence you need to fly without fear.

Pilot Briefing

How long before the flight do the crew arrive at the airport?

In the case of British Airways, the flight crew check-in time is 1 hour 15 minutes for short-haul flights and 1 hour 30 minutes for long haul. These timings may vary slightly from airline to airline but not by much. In practice, the pilots often arrive a lot earlier than that, especially if they have a long commute. Some even fly in as a passenger from overseas where they live. Some argue they would rather have an hour-and-a-half flight than a two-hour drive, and arrive at work more rested.

How do the crew prepare for the flight?

The first thing we do is to 'swipe in' using our electronic identity card through a special reader, which lets the company know we have arrived in time to operate the service. There is a complicated back-up system of standby crew at all times for both flight crew and cabin crew. Some crew will be at the airport, some in a nearby hotel and some on 'home standby', with a minimum report time of two hours. We all take it in turn to complete these standby duties, designed to protect the scheduled operation against sickness, travel disruption or anything else that might cause a crew member to be late to work such as a car breakdown.

Next we catch up on any recent notices from the company, which we can also do at home, and then request the paperwork for the flight. This is all prepared in advance by our flight technical dispatch department and comprises a plethora of information within several documents. In short, these documents show us our planned flight route; how much fuel we need (see Chapter 1, page 18); what the weather is like at departure, destination, and any airport we would ever be likely to use as a diversion along the route; areas of forecast turbulence or thunderstorm activity; any deficiencies with the aircraft or airports; a list of the crew members and a whole lot more besides.

After a short introduction and exchange of pleasantries, since we might never have met before, we take all of the above into consideration and decide whether to take the recommended and safe minimum fuel, or whether to take extra fuel on top.

The cabin crew carry out their own briefing, including being asked some safety questions, possibly in the form of an emergency scenario. At some point in our respective briefings we come together to make introductions and exchange any relevant information.

After proceeding through security, we aim to arrive at the aircraft between 40 minutes to one hour before the flight to make all the necessary preparations, such as loading the navigation computer and calculating our take-off speeds.

Check-in

Meanwhile, while all this is going on, you will be dropping your baggage at the airport having checked in either previously online, electronically at the airport, or in person at a desk. You will then proceed through security, where first of all you will need to produce your boarding card, and then you will have your hand baggage checked. Regulations vary from country to country but generally this will mean having no liquids, gels or creams greater than 100ml (3.5 fl oz) in quantity. Any that you wish to carry on board have to be placed in a small plastic bag and removed from your hand baggage. Laptops and tablet computers should also be removed and so should any metallic objects such as heavy watches, belts or shoes. These all go in a tray, which is then passed through an X-ray scanning machine. You will then be asked to walk through a metal archway also checking for metallic objects. Be patient, it's for your own safety!

Boarding

Keep an eye on the departure screens and around 45 minutes before departure time you will be asked to proceed to the gate and then, after producing your boarding card again, down to the aircraft. This is achieved by a variety of means, either by a jetty, the tube you walk down from the main terminal to the aircraft door, or by boarding a bus. After a final check of your boarding card by the cabin crew at the aircraft door, you will have made it on board! Any anticipatory anxiety will probably be at its peak by now, so employ the techniques that Patricia will cover in the second half of this book.

Your seat number is on your boarding card and usually written on the storage rack above your seat. Depending on whether you boarded first or last, there may be quite a wait while all the passengers get to their seats, the cargo and baggage is loaded, and all the paperwork is finalised. You may see a 'red cap' walking up and down to the flight deck if you are flying with British Airways. This is the dispatcher, responsible for coordinating all the pre-flight activity to ensure an on-time departure. All airlines have someone like this responsible for coordinating the departure process, everything from cleaning, loading, boarding and preparation of the loadsheet, but not all have a red cap!

There will be several announcements by the cabin crew welcoming you on board and you will be asked to turn off your mobile and fasten your seat belt. It's not too late to nip to the loo at this point if you need to.

When you get to the check-in desk, the aircraft door and especially at your seat, let one of the customer service staff know you are an anxious flyer. They will always be happy to help.

Push back

As you settle into your seat you will notice the sound of the air conditioning and you may notice the cabin lighting momentarily flicker as the electric supply is switched from the ground supply to the on-board auxiliary power unit (APU) by the pilots. The aircraft is usually pushed backwards from the parking stand by a heavy tug, with a driver and a pushback operative who is in communication with the flight crew via a headset plugged into the nose wheel.

Just before you push back, or have started to push back, you will hear the noise from the air conditioning diminish as the air from the APU is used for starting the engines. Very shortly after the aircraft begins to move backwards, and sometimes before, the cabin crew will be asked to 'place doors to automatic and cross check'. This is a standard call and it means that the inflatable slides are now armed should it be necessary to evacuate the aircraft in an emergency on the ground. Before the aircraft moves, you may hear the noise of the flaps being extended for take-off.

Taxiing

Once the engines have been started, the headset operative disconnected and moved clear and the flight crew have permission from air traffic control, the aircraft will move under the power of its own engines. *Aircraft like being in the air, not on the ground*, so the taxi out to the runway will sometimes be bumpier than any turbulence you may or may not experience!

Safety demonstration

Before departure, the flight crew give a safety demonstration detailing the following:

- Seatbelts. How to fasten them and when they should be worn – at all times when the seatbelt sign is illuminated. Often the airline recommend keeping your seatbelt fastened throughout the flight in case of turbulence.
- The location of emergency exits. In some cases your nearest exit may be behind you. Also they will point you to the existence of floor-level lighting to guide you to your nearest exit.
- In the event of a loss of air, oxygen masks will automatically drop down in front of you. You will be shown how to operate the oxygen mask and to secure your own mask first before assisting another person or child.
- The location of life vests. How to put on the life vest and inflate it.
- The location of the safety card, which contains all this information.

After the safety demonstration is finished a final check will be made by the cabin crew that everyone has their seatbelt on before you hear the announcement 'cabin crew take seats for take-off'. After this announcement, the pilots are informed that the cabin is ready for take-off, and some time later the next noise you will hear will be a repeated high-low chime as the flight crew indicate to the cabin crew that the aircraft is about to take off.

Take-off

Take-off is always noisy. *Noisy engines on take-off is a good sign that they are working well.* The aircraft accelerates down the runway and you will feel that acceleration. For short-haul aircraft, you will be airborne within around 45 seconds or less, and for long-haul aircraft it can be almost double that.

> Noisy engines on take-off is a good sign that they are working well.

Today, 100 per cent of take-offs are manually flown using an auto-throttle. The flight crew will be calm and monitoring the instruments closely for any abnormalities. On larger aircraft, a V1 speed will be announced at which, if any problem occurs, it will be safer to continue the take-off. At the calculated take-off speed, 'rotate' will be called and the handling pilot will gently raise the aircraft into the air.

WHAT CAUSES THAT SINKING FEELING AT TAKE-OFF?

The increase in pitch during take-off causes an increase in gravity ('g' force), which in turn creates a sinking feeling on your body. The pilots are experiencing exactly the same sensation, the difference being that they are expecting it as they are causing it. This is a perfectly normal sensation and will quickly pass as the aircraft establishes a steady pitch angle for climb out.

The next thing to happen is that the gear is raised; this is accompanied by the sound of the undercarriage doors opening, the wheels locking into place in the belly of the aircraft and a reassuring clunk as the gear doors lock into place. You may be able to hear this inside the cabin but, overall, the vibration caused by the drag of the undercarriage will decrease as the aircraft becomes more 'clean'.

NOT LONG AFTER TAKE-OFF, IT SOMETIMES FEELS LIKE WE ARE SUDDENLY DROPPING AGAIN, WHICH IS REALLY FRIGHTENING. WHAT IS HAPPENING?

This is known as the noise abatement procedure, the point at which we reduce from take-off power setting to a lesser climb setting. The problem with the human body is that your senses are designed to work on the ground, but don't work well in the air. The reason that you are able to maintain an upright posture with your eyes closed on the ground is because of the human balance system, buried deep in your inner ears. Sensors called otoliths in your inner ears sense *acceleration*.

As the aircraft accelerates at a standard rate from lift-off to the power reduction at around 1,000 feet (305 metres) above the ground, your otoliths return to a neutral position, ready for the next event. Thus, as the power is reduced and the aircraft continues to accelerate, but now at a slower rate, your ears detect this as a deceleration, and therefore a descent. Coupled with the reduction in engine noise you hear, it is natural that you are convinced that the aircraft is descending, when actually it is not, it is just *accelerating at a reduced rate*.

This effect is most noticeable on a twin-engined aircraft, or when maximum take-off power is being used for some other reason. The pilots feel the same sensation, but they are looking at their instruments telling them what is actually happening.

Climb

The aircraft continues to climb, usually in series of steps as it fits into the air traffic control pattern. Each time you level off, you will feel the same sensation as described above as the aircraft levels off and less engine power is required to maintain level flight. The flaps will be retracted in stages as the aircraft accelerates and less wing is required to produce the same lift. You will sometimes be able to hear this happening in the cabin.

Ears

I know that a few people worry about the pain that is experienced in your ears, which first starts when you are climbing or descending. There are lots of things you can do to alleviate this, but first let's understand why it's happening. It's all to do with pressurisation. As you climb, the amount of oxygen in the air decreases, and in order to keep the oxygen at an acceptable level to breathe normally, the aircraft is pressurised. This is done automatically during the climb using air from the engines and air conditioning machines called 'packs'.

As the pressure changes in the cabin, the air in your inner ear has to adjust to the pressure around you. This can happen very easily in most people, without any assistance, but for some, and especially if you are suffering from a cold or anything that may cause inflammation inside your ears, the adjustment in pressure is not so easily achieved, causing discomfort and, in extreme cases, severe pain.

The easiest way to equalise the pressure is to close your mouth, pinch your nose and breathe out hard, but that can also be quite painful. If you are prone to this condition, it is far better to take some decongestant tablets a couple of hours before the flight, and during the climb and descent to have a sweet to suck or a drink to sip, as the act of swallowing also helps the ears to equalise. Even if you are unable to equalise during the descent, don't panic: your ears will naturally adjust some time after landing.

Cruise

Many nervous flyers hate the take-off and landing but a significant number of people find the long, level segment in between take-off and landing, called the cruise, the hardest time to relax. The common theme here seems to be the fear of suddenly dropping uncontrollably. I hope that by understanding how an aircraft flies and the whole concept of lift (see Chapter 1, page 10), you are convinced that this simply can't happen. Remember: *the aircraft is constantly supported by lift from the wings and that cannot go away.*

During the cruise, pilots are constantly monitoring the flight instruments. They are in continuous radio contact with air traffic control as they fly from the airspace of one country to another and are passed to the next radio frequency. They are flying and navigating the aircraft through the autopilot and on-board navigation computers, which mostly use GPS signals from satellites and are incredibly accurate.

Remember that the pilots will also constantly be prepared for a diversion should the need arise, perhaps for a medical emergency on board. In order to be prepared, they will be continually checking the weather at the nearest airfields along the route and assessing the suitability of the airfield for a diversion. If the flight is over nine hours or so, depending on the time of the day, there will be three pilots and one will be resting so that they do not become tired.

Descent

Around 100 miles (160 km) from destination, the on-board computer calculates a top of descent point and, after clearance from air traffic control, the descent is commenced. As with the climb, the aircraft will descend in stages as it fits into the air traffic control flow, and, as the aircraft levels off each time, the opposite effect will be felt to that in the climb. Your ears, which will have returned to a neutral position, will detect the level off as a climb and this is supported by an increase in engine power.

Approach

Around half an hour before landing, the cabin crew will begin to 'secure' the cabin, making sure everyone is strapped in and all the cabin equipment is secure. This is entirely normal because you do not want people walking around when you land, as they might fall over when the aircraft brakes are applied. There is a lot of momentum to slow down, so the aircraft brakes quite hard initially. This could cause cabin equipment to fall and injure someone so it all has to be safely stowed away and the cabin crew need time to make sure that everything is ready for landing.

The flight crew will constantly be assessing their descent against the ideal approach path, making adjustments as necessary. The flaps will be extended as the aircraft decelerates, enabling the aircraft to fly more slowly. Around 2,000 feet (610 metres) above the ground, the landing gear will be lowered, causing a significant increase in noise and vibration.

All the landing checks will be completed by 1,000 feet (305 metres) and around 98 per cent of landings are manually flown to maintain the flight crew skill levels. The remaining 2 per cent of landings are autolands, for landing in fog or for practising the slightly different procedure we use when auto landing.

Landing

This is the most involved part of the flight for us, but always well within our capabilities. Much time is spent from day one of pilot training, perfecting our landing technique and each time we convert on to a new aircraft, firstly in the simulator. It's important to remember that a good landing is not necessarily silky smooth, as long as it is in the right place, at the right speed.

At touchdown, you may see the speedbrakes extend on the top of the wing and hear reverse thrust applied, but by far the biggest retardation comes from the brakes, which have advanced antiskid capability. Take a look at the image below of the wing just after landing clearly showing the land flap and speedbrakes fully extended. At a slow taxi speed the aircraft will be taxied off the runway, and the flaps and speedbrakes retracted.

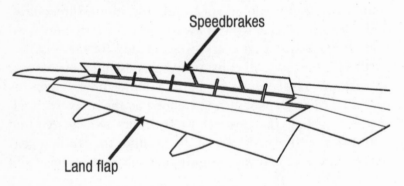

The wing just after landing clearly showing the land flap and speedbrakes fully extended.

Parking and shutdown

Sometimes, one or more of the engines will be shut down on the taxi in, which you may notice in the cabin. The

Auxiliary Power Unit (APU) is started, ready to take over air conditioning and electrics once the engines have been shut down after parking. The aircraft is either marshalled on to the stand with a 'bat man' or by using electronic guidance.

There can be a short delay as the jetty or steps are positioned at the aircraft side before the doors can be opened. After disembarking, you will be able to make your way through passport control, reclaim your baggage and go through customs.

In summary

I hope that, having been taken through a typical flight, you are now aware of what the pilots and the cabin crew do, the process you undergo when boarding an aircraft and what happens on a flight – including the physical sensations you experience during take-off and landing – and the technical aspects of flight. This should put you in a good frame of mind when you take your next journey: you will understand that the noises you hear – and the turbulence that you will probably encounter – is normal and nothing to worry about. Here are some other things to keep in mind when flying:

- The pilots and cabin crew come on board early for a briefing, and run through a series of checks before the flight.
- Any noise you hear is perfectly normal and is part of the flight. Take-off, for instance, is always noisy.
- The physical sensations you experience, such as a sudden drop just after take-off, is due to the physiological effects of being in the air, rather than on land, and is natural and nothing to worry about.

- Sip a drink or suck sweets during the ascent – this will help to alleviate the pressure in your ears.
- Landing is something that the pilots are experienced in. In fact, pilots take pride in landing an aircraft as safely as they can.

CHAPTER 9

CONCLUSION

My objective in this section has been to address one of the most fundamental causes for a fear a flying: a lack of knowledge. Scientist Madame Marie Curie once stated, 'Nothing in life is to be feared, it is merely to be understood.'

In this section, you have learnt about lift and how it enables an aircraft to fly, how it takes off, climbs, turns and lands. You have also learnt that the flight crew are carefully selected, highly trained and regularly re-trained and tested. You have learnt that turbulence is uncomfortable but never dangerous, no matter how bumpy your flight is, and that aircraft go up and down a few feet in turbulence, but never just keep dropping.

You should now understand how and why the pilots change the size of the wing to create more lift for take-off and landing. This is just one of the many routine actions that pilots do that create a noise or sensation that you can hear or feel in the cabin. All are perfectly normal and, unless you hear otherwise from the flight crew, everything is always happening as usual.

You have learnt that the balance system inside your inner ear has evolved over millions of years to work really well on the ground but not in the air and, therefore, every time you level off in the climb or descent in an aircraft, your ears do not really understand what is happening. Likewise in a turn, your eyes will misjudge the actual amount of bank. What can you do?

Trust the pilots. If in doubt, ask them! They will always be happy to reassure you. If you are on a long-haul BA jet, there is even an 'on demand' video within the In-Flight Entertainment system that will help you fly with confidence.

Having read all of this section you should now have more of an appreciation of what civil aviation is all about: well-trained pilots, immaculately maintained aircraft and a rigorous set of rules that govern each and every aspect of flying.

Think of the information I have given you as a toolkit. Many of you will be reading this book because you want to change your attitude towards flying, just like the thousands of people who have attended our courses over the past 25 years. The success of the British Airways Flying with Confidence course results largely from the attendees wanting to change their attitude, and therefore actually using the tools that we provide them with.

You must now do the same. Use the information in this section to help you relax on board, safe in the knowledge that the aircraft is extremely well maintained, the pilots are extremely well trained, and that flying really is the safest form of travel.

You should now feel reassured that no matter how bad the weather, your flight crew will have carefully considered their options and will *always* have your safety and security as their first priority. It is worth remembering that they themselves are just normal people, with families, spouses or partners, and have every expectation that they will return home safely after their day's work.

Some years ago, before mobile phones, I was in the middle of running one of our courses when, during a break, I nipped to a line of public telephones to ring my wife. I told her we were running a little late and asked her if she wouldn't mind getting my clothes ready for a dinner party later that evening. I noticed out of the corner of my eye another gentleman on the phone. Later in the day, after successfully completing the course, he explained to me that when I had seen him earlier he had been ringing his wife to come and pick him up because he couldn't go through with it. He had noticed me in uniform and overheard my conversation. He suddenly realised that I was already planning my evening and that everything was going to be all right on the flight! He changed his attitude there and then by realising that we go to work every day fully expecting to come back!

It is also worth remembering that, as pilots, we all love our jobs. We love flying: it is, for most of us, what we always dreamt of doing to earn our living. I look at the photo below with immense pride, and awe. We use this photograph on the Flying with Confidence course and, quite recently, I temporarily lost my flow when this slide appeared during my presentation. Without really thinking, I simply declared, 'That's my baby,' and moved on.

A Boeing 747 in flight.

Later in the day, I was embraced by a lady who had successfully completed the course, having arrived in the morning adamant that she would not be able to board the aircraft. She thanked me profusely, and then told me that the turning point was when that slide of the 747 had appeared and she had recognised the genuine love and affection I felt for 'my baby'.

It was like a light-bulb moment for her, a suddenly realisation that aircraft need not be seen as a threat to life or something to be afraid of, but as a thing of beauty, an incredible feat of engineering and a great way to travel around this wonderful planet we live on.

Remember: *aeroplanes like being in the air, it is what they are designed for. Pilots like being in the air, it is what we have always dreamt of.* My sincere hope is that if this book, in some small way, can help you to be more comfortable in the air, then, together, we have truly achieved something very precious indeed.

PART TWO

THE PSYCHOLOGICAL TOOLS FOR MASTERING YOUR FEARS

Patricia Furness-Smith:
psychologist and specialist in flying phobias

Each one of us has fears – it's an inevitable consequence of living in the world – but we can choose to be bullied by our fears, or face them. Life is too short to be restricted by your irrational thoughts and, as far as we know for certain, we only get one shot at it, so don't waste it. By picking up this book, you have chosen to change your life and have taken a big step towards overcoming your fear or phobia of flying.

Steve has already explained to you the mechanics of flight, how the aircraft is built to withstand any weather conditions and what it takes to become a pilot, and hopefully this has helped to quell some of your anxieties surrounding flight. In this section, I will explore the psychological side to your fear of flying. Over the next few chapters, my aim is to explain exactly what phobias are, what causes them, what goes on inside your brain when you experience them and, most importantly, what effective strategies you can use for overcoming them.

As someone with over 20 years' experience as a psychologist dealing with phobias, and also, incidentally, someone who spent their gap year working as an air stewardess, I have worked extensively with nervous flyers to develop effective methods of dealing with the acute anxiety experienced when stepping on to an aircraft. This range of techniques I call the four 'R's: *react, regulate, relax* and *rehearse*; these are the tools to help you manage your fear.

This part also includes a progressive relaxation exercise to help keep you calm and a guided visualisation of a trip to the airport and flight, which will give your brain a positive guideline to follow every time you are due to fly. Finally, I have some simple tips to bear in mind when flying and information on further help available.

Hopefully, what may have once seemed totally insurmountable will, thanks to the contents of this book, arm you with all the technical knowledge and a range of psychological techniques you need to help control your feelings of anxiety and enable you to conquer your fear of flying.

The only thing we have to fear is fear itself.

Franklin D. Roosevelt's First Inaugural Address

PHOBIAS AND FEARS

M any of you reading this book will have acknowledged that you have a phobia or know someone
close to you who has one. I feel it is very
important for the reader to gain a sound
comprehension of this phenomenon, as a lack of understanding can further fuel the phobia's domination over us.

What is a Phobia?

Very simply, a phobia is a persistent, irrational fear of a
specific situation, action, person, creature, concept or thing
that interferes with the way someone chooses to live their
life. To have a phobia, you technically need to meet the
following five basic requirements.

Your fear is:

1. Persistent
2. Abnormal, unreasonable, irrational, extreme
3. Targeted towards a specific type of person/object/creature/
   concept/situation/action
4. Engendering avoidance behaviour
5. A learned emotional response

Before we look further into phobias, it is helpful to first
consider that phobia is a type of fear.

Fear

Quite simply, fear is a very powerful, negative emotion, which we experience when we perceive ourselves to be in danger. We have this emotion to enable us to react to threats and it is key to our survival, both as an individual and as a species. Once danger has been recognised, fear causes our fight-or-flight mechanism to kick in. In periods of excessive stress, e.g. when we are under threat or in danger, the brain releases a surge of adrenalin and other stress hormones into the body to prepare it for 'fighting' or 'running', thus enabling us to take the necessary action to protect ourselves. In some cases, a third response, that of freezing, is the most appropriate option depending upon the nature of the danger. This mechanism is not perfect but serves us well on the whole, although occasionally we misdiagnose something as being dangerous when it is perfectly harmless.

OCCASIONAL MISDIAGNOSIS OF THREAT

A good example of this is when a friend comes up from behind and taps you on the shoulder to attract your attention and you nearly leap out of your skin.

PERMANENT MISDIAGNOSIS OF THREAT

Later in this chapter you will see that a phobia is just a specific fear. However, the important thing to grasp is that a phobia is not a helpful fear, such as described above, which serves to enhance our survival chances. A phobia is fundamentally an irrational fear, which does nothing to advance our survival and actively limits and curtails our options, which in turn compromises the quality of our lives. One aspect of a phobia is there is *always* a permanent misdiagnosis of threat based upon an irrational premise. People have phobias about many things such as trees, crossing bridges, and clowns, to name a few common ones. This is not to say that there would never be such a thing as a falling tree, collapsing bridge or homicidal clown, all of which have the potential to be dangerous. However, to always avoid the above in the firm conviction that they are *all* dangerous is not a sound risk assessment to say the least.

> **A phobia is always a misdiagnosis of threat.**

Types of phobias

The fascinating thing about phobias is their sheer diversity. However, it is possible to roughly divide them into several major types as follows:

1. **Animal phobias:** e.g. fear of snakes, cats, moths, rats, bats, fish, birds, wolves, bees, horses, spiders, sharks and worms.
2. **Natural environment phobias:** e.g. fear of water, snow, wind, lightning, darkness, heights, clouds, fog, dust particles, sunlight, trees, dirt, flowers, fruit, earthquakes, sounds and fire.
3. **Body-based phobias:** e.g. fear of vomiting, insanity, blood, belly buttons, hands, fatigue, cancer, pain, faeces, rabies, hair, becoming cold, bad breath, being touched, sleep, germs, medications, becoming too hot, choking, sweating, death, disease, coughing, sneezing, being injected, being injured and blood transfusion.
4. **People phobias:** e.g. fear of clowns, dentists, homosexuals, lepers, particular nationalities, foreigners, a particular race, bisexuality, those with learning difficulties/amputations/

disfigurements/visual impairments/obesity, transgender, women, men, lesbians, transsexuals and the elderly.

5. **Actions or situational phobias:** e.g. a fear of flying, walking, going to the dentist, descending stairs, having an operation, giving birth, going in lifts, taking the tube, travelling on motorways, crossing bridges, entering enclosed spaces.

6. **Social phobias:** e.g. a fear of eating or drinking in public, signing cheques in public, meeting people, public speaking, being stared at, being photographed, crowds, making phone calls, attending interviews.

7. **Concepts and things phobias:** e.g. a fear of numbers, dates, months, colours, foods, ghosts, aliens, buttons, seams, being buried alive, computers, losing things, bubbles, velvet, cotton wool and bubble wrap.

8. **Agoraphobia:** a fear of open spaces or unfamiliar territory (see below).

Having a fear of flying is classed as a specific situational phobia.

Agoraphobia

Agoraphobia enjoys a category all of its own. This is because it actually develops as a result of the fear of panic attacks. Hence the trigger is any situation in which an agoraphobic feels escape may be difficult. The person's horizons become more and more limited until they cannot leave the security and familiarity of their own home. In some extreme cases, they can only endure being at home if permanently accompanied by a familiar companion.

Simple or complex phobia

Phobias can also be classified as 'simple' or 'complex'. A fear of flying technically qualifies as a simple phobia, since it is a fear of a specific situation. However, due to the fact that it can also co-exist with other fears, such as agoraphobia and claustrophobia (a fear of enclosed spaces and being closed-in), it can also be categorised as a complex phobia. An example of this would be someone suffering from claustrophobia struggling to walk down the jet-bridge as well as having a fear of flying for a variety of other reasons.

Why do phobias appear?

There are a number of ways that we develop phobias and these can include the following:

1. *By observation*: such as witnessing a hysterical sibling screaming while being dragged to the dentist or hearing a terrified parent shriek at the sight of a mouse.
2. *By being indoctrinated or told repeatedly about a potential danger*: such as a friend or colleague who is neurotic about cleanliness and interminably talks about the likelihood of contamination if someone sneezes or coughs in close proximity. Or a young person who is told that they must be eternally vigilant in watching out for poisonous spiders whenever they step out of doors.
3. *By direct experience resulting in trauma*: such as being stung by a wasp and suffering an anaphylactic shock or being trapped in a lift for several hours feeling over heated and terrified that you will not be discovered.
4. *By a false alarm*: such as when we have misjudged an innocuous situation as a threat. For example, being followed by someone who merely wanted to reunite us

with the wallet we dropped but we construed the situation as a potential attack. Or hearing a noise in the night that we believed to be caused by an intruder, but turns out to be something falling off the washing machine due to the vibrations caused by the spin cycle.

5. *By experiencing too much stress:* such as when events and circumstances make demands upon us that we are unable to meet. We are built to withstand various levels of stress since no existence could ever be totally stress-free. However, we are all unique and possess different levels of coping ability. These are our inherent resources or lack of them, the latter of which constitutes our Achilles heel.

To find out more on exactly how phobias are formed and what is going on inside the brain, see Chapter 11, page 111.

Why can some people cope with more stress than others?

Stress is an interesting phenomenon as it can be both a positive and a negative factor in our life. Without enough stress some of us are at risk of 'rust-out'. This is where a lack of being stretched or stimulated can cause anxiety and depression. For example, when a previously busy executive retires and feels bored trying to fill up their day with mundane tasks such as shopping, tidying cupboards, etc., life can start to feel meaningless and superficial. As a result they can suffer psychological disturbance. Whereas for others, the greater danger is that of 'burn-out', which is the result of the demands being put upon us exceeding our personal resources to meet those demands.

So stress can be a motivator for us to stretch ourselves by making changes, finding solutions or producing a peak performance but too much stress can overwhelm our resources causing us resultant problems. Ultimately, our capability of how much stress we can cope with is determined by our ability to find the right balance. Being stretched causes brain cells in the hippocampus, the part of the brain that plays an important role in the consolidation of information, to increase and memory function to improve, whereas being stressed causes them to deteriorate and memory function to decline.

PHYSICAL MANIFESTATIONS RESULTING FROM TOO MUCH STRESS

For some people, the outcome of too much stress may manifest itself in a physical manner resulting in complaints such as back ache, irritable bowel syndrome (IBS), skin disorders, ulcers and migraines to name but a few.

PSYCHOLOGICAL MANIFESTATIONS RESULTING FROM TOO MUCH STRESS

For others, our mental health is affected and we may develop any of a range of disorders such as general anxiety disorder (GAD), obsessive-compulsive disorder (OCD), depression, drug or alcohol addictions, an eating disorder or, if we are fortunate, a phobia. I say fortunate, as phobias are highly treatable and can be dispatched very swiftly indeed.

Physical and psychological combos

It should be noted that many people who suffer from too much stress do not restrict themselves to one of the above disorders and frequently will suffer from a phobia along with say a touch of depression and IBS or migraines and perhaps an over-dependence on alcohol or cigarettes. Some of us may even own several imps (what I call phobias) but the good news is that they all can be managed or eradicated by using the techniques which I will explain in depth in Chapters 13–16.

Meet the Imp

Imagine your phobia as a mischievous little imp. The sole purpose of these small creatures from German folklore was to bug and harass humans by misleading them. They took great delight in causing mayhem through sabotage and the playing of tricks, jokes and pranks. An imp is not really a dangerous enemy, more like an irritating child that needs to be disciplined and controlled. This is particularly appropriate for a phobia, since – of all the psychological afflictions that may befall us – a phobia is one of the easiest to tackle and either manage or cure.

An imp: your phobia.

I find this analogy empowering because most adults feel that they are equipped to deal with naughty children. They certainly wouldn't allow a spoilt child to dictate to them and ultimately control, or even ruin, their life!

Initially, the manifestation of an imp is in some ways the body's cry for help, a signal that things cannot continue like this and some fundamental changes need to be put in place so that we do not continue to overload ourselves. However, if allowed, the imp will make itself at home, becoming a habit and overstaying its welcome long after measures have been put in place to address the original problem.

Remember the function of an imp is to mislead humans and that is exactly what your phobia is doing.

The disposition of an imp

It is worth commenting that some of us are genetically much more disposed to developing phobias (acquiring imps) than others. You will probably know someone that seems to thrive on risks and challenges. These individuals have high tolerance levels and hence need colossal amounts of stimulation to feel engaged in life. It takes an awful lot of stress before these types of people would offer a home to an imp as they are endowed with much greater levels of resilience.

Others have the tolerance bar set extremely low and it doesn't take much to tip them over into anxiety. As children, those who are more sensitive to stress would have been more likely to have been frightened of the dark and/or animals. They may have shown their anxious disposition by being bed wetters, nail biters and much more wary of any new experiences. People within this group deserve our esteem as every day they have to push themselves out of their comfort zone in order to compete in a world with others who are totally unfazed by the same demands and expectations. A good example is those who would sooner undergo root canal treatment than parade on a stage indulging in the joys of karaoke, whereas others cannot hit the stage fast enough. We all have very different resources.

Fear of Flying

Having given a broad outline of the generalities of phobias, it is now time to specifically look at the fear of flying, also known as aviaphobia, aviophobia, aviatophobia, aerophobia and pteromerhanophobia! (I did hesitate before including the latter out of fear of triggering someone's hippopoto-monstrosesquippedaliophobia, which is the fear of long words!)

Do you have a dislike of flying or a fear of flying phobia?

The key element to answering this question depends upon whether you organise your life around *avoiding* flying. As stated earlier in the chapter, a phobia or imp must also:

1. *Be persistent:* have you struggled with the idea of flying for some time?
2. *Be specific:* there is no doubt that flying is a specific situation that triggers the phobia.
3. *Be a learned response:* due to the fact that flying is a very recent phenomenon, it certainly falls into this category. Primitive man would not have been hardwired to avoid flying since this option did not previously exist.
4. *Be irrational:* it certainly ticks this box too as the following statistics will amply demonstrate.

> ## Did you know?
>
> According to the National Transportation Statistic Report carried out in 1985, flying is:
>
> - 29 times safer than travelling by car
> - 18 times safer than staying at home
> - 10 times safer than being at work
> - 8 times safer than walking down the street
> - 6 times safer than the possibility of being murdered by a relative
> - 4 times safer than travelling by train

Aerophobia is the Rolls-Royce of phobias

Now I admit that this is only my personal opinion but, as someone who has spent many years specialising in phobias, I have to confess that I find aerophobia the sexiest phobia of the lot. I have met literally thousands of people with this particular imp and not one of them has the same imp profile. Such a variety of different factors can go into this particular species of imp, which makes each person's phobia so fascinating and special.

> Just because a phobia can be made up of a number of components and combinations of other phobias, it does not mean it is more intransigent and difficult to manage or cure.

Here are some of the many potential components of aerophobia, some of which are phobias in their own right.

Acrophobia	fear of heights
Agoraphobia	fear of open spaces
Astrophobia	fear of thunder and lightning
Athenophobia	fear of fainting
Basophobia	fear of falling
Claustrophobia	fear of enclosed spaces
Coronary phobia	fear of a heart attack
Dementophobia	fear of losing one's mind (going mad)
Emetophobia	fear of vomiting (self or others)
Halitophobia	fear of having bad breath (close proximity)
Haphephobia	fear of being touched (invasion of privacy)
Hydrophobia	fear of water (crossing oceans)
Mysophobia	fear of germs
Nomophobia	fear of being out of mobile phone contact
Osmophobia	fear of odours
Phobophobia	fear of having a phobia
Phonophobia	fear of loud sounds
Sociophobia	fear of people
Scopophobia	fear of being looked at
Technophobia	fear of technology
Terrorphobia	fear of terrorism
Thanatophobia	fear of death
Truamatophobia	fear of injury
Xenophobia	fear of strangers or people from other countries

There are also other factors, which do not have a specific phobia name, that can be part of the profile of a person suffering from aerophobia. These are the fear of being separated from loved ones, crashing or a fear of panic attacks and suffocating.

Why People Develop Aerophobia

There are many reasons why people develop this condition. Here are some of the most common reasons:

1. People who have never flown before but are anxious about new experiences (this is technically being neophobic).
2. People who suffer from a low anxiety threshold and therefore find many sensations that feel unnatural as very threatening.
3. People who have been traumatised by an experience in which they perceived themself to be in danger, whether the threat was real or imagined.
4. People who have never been in an incident but have devoured other people's experiences and become vicariously traumatised. This group makes sure that they never knowingly miss any airline disaster movie and avidly read every accident report that they can lay their hands on. They are the sort of person that would go on *Mastermind* with 'Disasters' as their specialist topic. Although it would appear to be counter-intuitive to behave in this manner, those readers who are familiar with cognitive dissonance theory will understand why they do it.*
5. People who suffer from concomitant phobias, which have become progressively worse, and this then comingles with the aerophobia, e.g. those whose agoraphobia or claustrophobia has increased in strength.
6. People who have experienced higher levels of stress in the previous six months.

* In essence, this theory states that people feel fraught when they have thoughts or ideas that conflict with one another and therefore tend to seek to validate these thoughts to avoid this conflict. For example, you might feel that flying is dangerous and want to avoid it, yet feel upset as you know that many people fly safely and have wonderful holidays because of it. In order to feel less conflicted by this, you might focus on airline accidents and brush over safety statistics so you feel justified in your avoidance of air flight.

stress levels is by far the largest category it
nention. We are all familiar with stress in
the word that we usually apply to describe
the way ... nd to excessive demands being placed upon
us. When we feel under pressure, we say we are feeling
stressed. Many people are not aware that all changes bring
in their wake increased levels of stress, whether they are
good or bad changes.

CONSIDER THE FOLLOWING POSSIBILITIES:

Being made redundant
Getting married
Upgrading to a new home
Writing a book
Living in an unhappy marriage
Being bereaved
Best friend emigrates
Child goes off to university
Winning the lottery
Achieving a much sought-after promotion
Being fired from your job
Being bullied at work
Suffering from health problems
Meeting the partner of your dreams
Having an extension built on your property
Getting divorced
Passing your exams
Going on holiday
Being elected captain of your golf club
Helping your child prepare for an exam
Having children abroad on a gap year
HAVING YOUR FIRST CHILD

Supporting elderly parents
Achieving a personal best in a marathon
Struggling to pay your mortgage
Being pregnant
Getting a speeding ticket
Feuding with your neighbours
Putting on weight
Being nominated for an OBE
Joining a choir or amateur dramatics society

The list could go on and on but hopefully it will have contained sufficient possibilities to hopefully include some factors that are familiar to you. The point is that, although some of the above seem obvious vehicles of stress overload, such as being bullied, bereaved, divorced or made redundant, others, while less obvious, also take a tremendous psychological toll too.

Positive changes cause stress too

It's not just negative stress that can do some damage. Adjusting to new ways of living – whether it is taking on a promotion at work, winning the lottery, seeing your last child off to university or commencing retirement – exact a great deal of energy from us.

Familiarity in itself is a great energy saver as much of our daily behaviours are carried out on an autopilot basis, causing minimal psychological expenditure. When we make simple changes to our daily routines we have to learn and consciously implement new behaviours, which place a demand on our psyche. Remember the initial effort you had to exert in order to learn to drive competently. How often do you still have to consciously think 'mirror, signal, manoeuvre', or do you just find yourself at your destination having paid scant attention to the art of driving?

A Series of Small Changes can have a Big Effect

Try and look back at what was happening in your life in the six months or so before you acquired your flying imp (phobia). Even if it is a mixture of very small events, the cumulative effect can be enough to trigger the onset of a phobia.

Some of you may have noticed that 'Having your first child' in the list of stress triggers on page 106 was typed in capitals. This was done purely to pay homage to the fact that, in my empirical research, this is the single most dominant factor that appears to trigger aerophobia. In many ways, it is not surprising as we are programmed to protect the next generation and anything that is perceived as a threat to this intention will resonate in the primitive part of our brain, which is responsible for our survival.

Case history

Chantal had suffered from travel sickness since she was a small child. In the first year of her studies towards her Baccalaureate in France, she suffered horrendous humiliation while on a school trip to London. She had already felt nervous about leaving her parents for the first time and was concerned about how she would cope being away from them for two whole weeks. This anxiety was further exacerbated by her upset, two days prior to the trip's departure, when her small dog Fifi suffered a serious injury to her paw by treading on a shard of broken glass. During the Channel crossing, Chantal had felt very emotional and worried about her dog. Five minutes after returning to the coach in Dover, Chantal began to feel very unwell. She informed her teacher that she was feeling nauseous but was unsympathetically told to return to her seat. Despite her best efforts, Chantal was sick and the other children made no effort to hide their disgust. The following two weeks were pure agony for Chantal. She missed her parents desperately, worried about Fifi's recovery and had to put up with the relentless teasing from her classmates. Most of all, she was fearful about how she would cope with the return journey to Paris. Needless to say, with so much anxiety, coupled with her disposition to travel sickness, she suffered again on the return journey. Chantal was mortified.

As a result of this devastating experience Chantal refused to put herself into any situation where she would run the risk of being trapped if she felt unwell. Along with refusing to go to the cinema, theatre or opera unless her parents could secure aisle seats, Chantal resolutely refused to travel on any form of public transport, including aeroplanes. Despite being debilitated by her travel and social phobia, Chantal was successful in her school career and secured a place at the Sorbonne, where she achieved a first class honours degree.

During this time, Chantal met her future husband, Marco, an American graduate, studying for his doctorate in astrophysics in the UK. Marco, appreciating Chantal's difficulty with travelling, was happy to commute from London to Paris on a fortnightly basis; however, on achieving his PhD, he was offered a wonderful opportunity of work in Canada. He was eager to accept but only if his fiancée, Chantal, would accompany him. Knowing how much this job meant to Marco, she agreed to address her travel fears. Having successfully embarked on personal therapy locally, Chantal was able to take the metro, local buses and even the ferry to Dover. However, the thought of a long-haul flight to Canada still filled her with fear. She was not confident that she could tolerate so many hours on board without the opportunity of getting off should she feel unwell. I met Chantal five years ago and worked through her travel fears with her. She and Marco are now happily settled in Canada and frequently fly back to Paris to visit Chantal's family.

In summary

Having an understanding of a phobia is vital in helping you to not only come to terms with it but also overcome it. Knowing how such irrational fears can start to become your 'norm' is a positive step towards dealing with them. The good news is that all phobias, including aerophobia, are highly treatable and needn't hold you in their grasp for the rest of your life. Remember:

- Phobias are persistent, specific and irrational fears.
- Phobias are chiefly learned responses causing us to avoid the feared situation at all costs.
- Phobias are often the result of too much stress in our lives.
- Phobias can appear in isolation or with other physical and psychological conditions such as irritable bowel syndrome (IBS) and obsessive-compulsive disorder (OCD).
- Phobias are mostly a warning sign that our lives are not in balance and some emotional need should be addressed.
- Phobias, such as aerophobia, can be made up of many separate fears, such as fear of heights, vomiting and dying.
- The complexity of a phobia bears no relationship to its manageability or curability.

Don't settle for half a life, live life to the full.

CHAPTER 11

WHAT IS GOING ON IN YOUR BRAIN WHEN YOU HAVE A PHOBIA?

Your brain is an enigma – it enables you to be stronger, faster and more resourceful than you can possibly imagine but, alas, it can also render you deficient.

The Brain is Responsible for Your Fear

Phobias can be very distressing and confusing. You might be perfectly aware that your fear of flying is irrational; however, this doesn't mean that your imp won't act up at the prospect of flying – either making you very distressed about the flight or stopping you from taking the flight at all.

Throughout your life you can usually take control of your behaviour, acting to fulfil your own wants and needs. For example, when you feel dehydrated you can drink some water, thus quenching your thirst, or if you feel lonely you can call a friend for a chat. However, when you are in the grips of a phobia, you may find yourself unable to behave in the manner of your choosing. Your ability to take a certain course of action has been hijacked by your imp and you are left feeling disempowered, vulnerable and out of control. To understand how this can happen it is useful to give a basic explanation of how the brain works.

The three brains

We refer to the brain, somewhat unhelpfully, as a single organ. However, it is, in fact, made up of three distinct brains or systems. These three brains have developed at different points in our evolution and, although connected, they perform largely distinctive functions. These three parts are called the reptilian brain, the mammalian brain and the human brain.

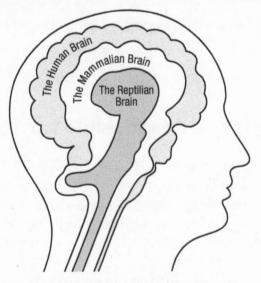

The parts of the brain.

THE REPTILIAN BRAIN (THE LOWER BRAIN, OR INSTINCTIVE BRAIN)

This is the most ancient structure of the brain. This primitive brain emerged many, many millions of years ago, forging an evolutionary link between dinosaurs and mammals. It is responsible for basic bodily functions such as controlling the body's thermostat, breathing, balance and heartbeat. It operates in an instinctual and ritualistic manner attending to survival needs, such as mating and protection of territory. The simple reptilian brain makes basic choices such as: does this food look edible or poisonous? It is this part of the brain that reacts with indignation and hostility when someone hogs the shared armrest of your cinema seat – known as 'the territorial imperative'.

THE MAMMALIAN BRAIN (THE LIMBIC SYSTEM, OR EMOTIONAL BRAIN)

This was the next brain to evolve. We have this brain in common with all other mammals. It is within this part of the brain that we form attachments to others and experience emotions. It is also responsible for attention, behaviour, motivation and our processing of smell. It is this part of the brain that reacts when certain smells or sounds suddenly catapult you back in time to a moment in your childhood. Most importantly for our purposes, emotionally charged memories of behaviour are also down to this part of the brain. For example, the memory of your last flight, if you experienced it as frightening, will be stored here. One of its key roles is to ensure our survival in the face of threat or danger.

THE HUMAN BRAIN (THE NEOCORTEX, OR THINKING BRAIN)

This was the final brain to evolve. This brain is responsible for our ability to use language, reason, make sense of our past experience and plan for our future. It is this part of the brain that enables us to perform complex, higher order mental functions – a feature that separates us from other mammals.

The three-bird roast

An easy way to visualise the three brains is to think of the familiar three-bird roast, which is often served at Christmas. One of the most popular versions is the pheasant within a chicken within a goose. In brain terms, the pheasant represents the ancient reptilian brain, which is surrounded by the chicken – the mammalian brain – and the goose represents the large and most recent part of the brain, the neocortex.

Meet General Amygdala

Most significant to phobias is an almond-shaped structure found in the mammalian brain called the amygdala. Its function is to continually scan your environment, seeking out any threat to your survival. If the amygdala discerns a threat it takes immediate action for our protection by firing the fight-or-flight response mechanism (see Chapter 10, page 94).

I find it a helpful device to think of the amygdala as the 'General'. In the same way that an army general is able to instantly mobilise the troops to ward off the enemy, the amygdala reacts in a similar fashion. Once the amygdala perceives that we are exposed to a threat, it fires the fight-or-flight response mechanism, which in turn causes our body's defences to be activated. It therefore makes sense that whenever we are in danger, the General should have instant supreme command. He is best placed to ensure our survival by mobilising an army of stress hormones. These hormones will prime our body to be physically able to exert the maximum muscular effort to defeat the enemy/threat.

The General – the amygdala.

The General (amygdala) always prefers to err on the side of caution, which is just as well from a survival point of view since it is far better to misdiagnose a danger when one doesn't exist than to miss one when the threat is real. The General uses a process known as 'pattern matching'. This involves the comparing of incoming stimuli/data to previously stored patterns or memories that have been filed away as threatening.

Most memories are deemed to be innocuous or safe and are filed elsewhere in the brain. However, the memories that relate to feeling threatened are considered key to our future survival, so are retained in the mammalian brain, along with the accompanying emotions they originally elicited. This is why you might find that a frightening incident, imbued with all its painful emotions, may be repeatedly experienced when triggered by incoming stimuli bearing the vaguest of resemblances to the original event. This is because this process works upon the principle of approximation, rather than an accurate, comprehensive match.

For example, if you were attacked by a Dobermann, the General (amygdala) would likely perceive all patterns roughly approximating a Dobermann – i.e. all canine forms – to be potentially threatening. Therefore, if an Alsatian, Labrador, spaniel or poodle approached you, the General would react

115

as though this dog were threatening, regardless of the intention or affability of the said hound. Similarly, you quickly learn that it is as well to be wary of all objects on four wheels moving at a fast pace, whether it be a mini or a lorry, after you have had an altercation with a van.

An example of how extreme this can be is someone who has been involved in a motoring accident. The stored patterns surrounding this incident could include noises, smells and sights. If the person then smells burning rubber while on a fairground ride on the dodgems this could trigger a pattern match. Equally, hearing the screech of brakes while watching a DVD of a high-speed chase could also trigger a pattern match. In both cases, the individual will be overwhelmed by a range of symptoms resulting from the General activating the fight-or-flight response mechanism.

The vital concept to grasp is that the process, described above, happens *unconsciously*; that is, it is outside of our conscious control. It is critical for the mammalian brain that, in moments of crisis, action is taken immediately. Otherwise it may be too late. For this reason we cannot afford the luxury of pondering about the situation and then deliberating on what we are going to do about it. Time is of the essence, and our very survival might well depend upon an instantaneous course of decisive action. This action is preferably to run away and if this is not possible then to fight the threat.

Meet the Cavalry

When the General (amygdala) decides that the body is facing a threat, he activates an alarm to the body. This is registered in the hypothalamus, the part of the brain that controls the autonomic nervous system (ANS), which sends an instant message to the adrenal glands. The glands then immediately emit stress hormones, including cortisol and adrenalin, which mobilise stored glucose to working muscles, shut down metabolic processes such as digestion to preserve energy and increase the heart and breathing rate and raise blood pressure to prepare the body for action. Together, they are known as the fight-or-flight hormones.

I find it is helpful to consider these stress hormones as the 'Cavalry' – a highly mobile, efficient, flexible and potent force that helps rescue the body from danger.

The Cavalry – the stress hormones

Meet the Sovereign

When we are not under threat we make conscious decisions and choices by means of the thinking part of the brain, the neocortex. I like to refer to the neocortex as the 'Sovereign'.

Just as a wise sovereign rules the kingdom by means of conscious rational decisions, so too the neocortex governs our behaviour in this measured manner.

To weigh up all the pros and cons of a situation inevitably takes time. This is fine in times of peace, since our survival is not in jeopardy. However, in times of war, a wise ruler delegates powers so that instant decisions can be made without any unnecessary delay.

The Sovereign – the neocortex.

Both the neocortex and the amygdala receive information and both parts of the brain process the incoming stimuli and communicate with each other to a certain extent. I say to a certain extent, since there are infinitely more pathways going from the General (amygdala) to the Sovereign (neocortex) than connections going from the Sovereign to the General.

Unconscious control

Basically, the voice of the General (amygdala) is stronger and louder and the amplified volume drowns out and dominates the Sovereign, the thinking part of the brain. If no powerful emotions are engaged, such as fear in the face of threat, the General will happily acquiesce to the Sovereign's rule and remain docile. The result of this state of affairs is that when emotions are running high, the General has the upper hand and is therefore in charge. Once the General has taken command and has given the order for '*short-term-survival*' mode to be implemented, a metaphorical trap-door closes, thus denying access to the thinking part of the brain and we proceed to operate under unconscious emotional control until the danger has passed.

Frequently when asked the question, 'How did you know what to do?' people who have been in an emergency situation will reply, 'I didn't think, it was just pure instinct.' Although, strictly speaking, instinct is not the correct term, they are quite right in stating that they didn't have to think as in effect the firing of the fight-or-flight mechanism had instantly switched them over to *unconscious control*.

Overuse of the fight-or-flight response mechanism

People who possess an overly sensitive amygdala will perceive more situations as threatening and this, in turn, will be interpreted as the world being a frightening and dangerous place. The constant activation of the fight-or-flight mechanism actually serves to alter the brain structure and thus a vicious cycle is set up causing the General (amygdala) to become trigger-happy, perceiving innocuous events as threatening.

We have all heard the expression 'use it or lose it', which is why many of us exercise our brains (the neocortex, to be precise) with mental arithmetic, puzzles, playing chess, etc., in order to keep it up to scratch. In exactly the same way, constant use of the fight-or-flight response mechanism strengthens this process. This is, of course, fine when a real threat appears but is very destructive when fired off at the drop of a hat, since it is both exhausting and demoralising for the individual. This is how activities that you could previously do easily, such as take a flight, travel in the tube, drive on the motorway or get into a lift, become monumental challenges. Life becomes a roller-coaster existence and the individual feels utterly out of control and frightened by their body, which seems to have a will of its own, due to operating under unconscious control.

Shakespeare rather uncharitably ascribed this phenomenon

as being caused by cowardice, when he described people who are constantly fearful for their existence as follows:

Cowards die many times before their deaths;
The valiant never taste death but once.

Julius Caesar, William Shakespeare

We now know that courage or cowardice is more than the disposition of our personality and also involves the current status of our brain's chemistry and structures. Some people are born with a highly anxious disposition, which causes them to be naturally overly sensitive to danger. For others, it is a learned response, resulting from a previous frightening experience, real or otherwise.

Example of the learned response

If you fall into the latter category when it comes to aerophobia, the following may have taken place:

1. You had a very turbulent flight.
2. You did not understand that turbulence was harmless and felt very frightened by the experience.
3. Your General (amygdala) read the situation as being a serious threat to your survival.
4. He logged all the data, including sensations, sounds, smells, tastes and sights surrounding the incident, to enable him to be able to identify any future pattern matches to ensure your on-going safety.
5. Any mention of anything remotely connected with flying will cause the General to instantly warn you off participating in this pursuit. This is why you might feel upset when booking your holiday, being presented with a meal similar to that offered on the flight, packing your case or even just hearing an aircraft overhead.

6. He will continue to give you plenty of warnings, via a weak cocktail of stress hormones, that flying is something that is not in your best interest and should be avoided at all costs. Thus you will experience some very uncomfortable anticipatory anxiety, particularly during the 24 hours prior to your flight.

7. If you do not heed his warnings and proceed to take a flight, he will interpret this as you putting yourself in the way of grave danger. He will then proceed to short-term emergency survival mode by activating the fight-or-flight response mechanism, which will cause you to be deluged with stress hormones.

Later in the book we will explore the symptoms, which are expressed while the body is under short-term emergency survival mode, and we will see that they are both uncomfortable and frightening. The antidote to the over-zealous General lies in our ability to develop the art of relaxation. This will enable us to handle stressful situations more constructively, which, in turn, will reset or recondition the amygdala's base level of stimulation.

Case history

Saleem's job involved him having to fly on a regular basis back and forth from Brussels to Perth. He had always enjoyed the travelling element of his work and had never experienced any anxiety with regard to flying. Saleem productively used the time on board the flight to prepare for his meetings and catch up on the latest films offered on the in-flight entertainment. He would then settle down and sleep for several hours to ensure that he arrived at his destination feeling relaxed and refreshed.

This pattern continued for eight years until, four years ago, when returning home to Brussels, Saleem believed himself to be in danger. The aeroplane had almost completed its descent for landing when suddenly it started to climb once more. Many passengers gasped at this unexpected event and Saleem became exceedingly distressed. He recalls that his throat became very dry and his heart felt as though it was racing. His breathing accelerated and beads of sweat formed on his brow. He recalls that his overriding feeling was of absolute terror and he desperately wanted to get out of the situation.

Fairly soon after the missed approach, the captain announced that air traffic control had instructed him to enact the go-around procedure. These discontinued approaches are fairly routine for pilots and they are well trained to deal with them, as explained in Chapter 7. It is not always possible for pilots to explain ahead what is about to happen and they prioritise in the following order: aviate; navigate; communicate.

Although there had been no real threat, Saleem's General (amygdala) had interpreted the unexpected situation as dangerous. As a consequence of this erroneous assessment, the signal to prepare for short-term emergency survival mode was given, resulting in Saleem's body being flooded by adrenalin and other stress hormones. Since he was not in a position to flee or fight the situation, Saleem spent the next 15 minutes, until the aeroplane safely landed, in a state of painful agitation.

On returning home, Saleem reflected on the incident and was both shocked and embarrassed, as he believed his reaction to be ludicrously out of proportion with what had actually taken place. As the days drew closer for Saleem to book his next flight, he found himself reluctant to do so. His anxiety persisted to such an extent that he found himself making up an excuse to his employer of why he should not fly to Perth. His avoidance tactics continued for several months until he eventually felt compelled to request a transfer in the company to a role involving no overseas travel. Saleem settled down in his new role, relieved at first that he *no longer had to fly. This relief gave way to resentment when he eventually acknowledged to himself how much he had sacrificed as he had loved his old job. This was the turning point and Saleem sought help to reclaim his confidence in flying.*

For the last three and a half years, Saleem has been working for a new company in a role that requires a considerable amount of international travel. He has totally recovered his ability to fly with confidence and is currently working towards achieving his private pilot's licence.

> Just like a caring parent, your brain can be overly protective. Although this is well intentioned, it is nonetheless a nuisance.

In summary

I hope this explanation of how the brain works has answered some of your questions as to why you have been unable to achieve something that you really wanted to do, such as take a flight. By understanding that your survival mechanism has unconsciously kicked in, on account of your General (amygdala) mistakenly reading the situation as threatening while pattern matching, is reassuring as you now understand why you behave in a manner that is quite the opposite of what your conscious mind intends, that is to take a flight to enjoy a holiday with your family. Understanding how your brain works is important to understanding your phobia.

- The brain can be described as a triadic structure in accordance with its evolutionary development.

- The first brain to evolve is the reptilian brain, which is instinctual and attends to our basic survival needs.
- The second brain to evolve is the mammalian brain, which is emotional and plays a key role in our survival when we are under threat.
- The third brain to evolve is the human brain (the neocortex), which is a thinking brain enabling us to be creative, analytical and logical as well as able to use language.
- The General (my name for the part of the brain called the amygdala) is your personal protection officer and is located in the mammalian brain. He uses a process known as pattern matching, which can lead to the activation of the fight-or-flight response mechanism to help ensure our survival. This part of the brain is not under conscious control.
- The Cavalry refers to the release of stress hormones into the blood stream, which prepares the body to be able to mount a powerful physical reaction to threat.
- The erroneous activation of the fight-or-flight response mechanism can only be recalibrated by long-term practice of relaxation.
- The Sovereign (the part of the brain known as the neocortex) performs executive functions and is in command apart from times of high emotional agitation. This part of the brain operates under conscious control.

CHAPTER 12

BEING IN THE RIGHT MINDSET FOR OVERCOMING YOUR FEARS

In order for you to successfully overcome the challenge of your phobia, it is vital that you feel fully prepared and are fit and able to face the problem head on. While it's important you have acknowledged you have an irrational fear, there's no point wasting valuable time and energy beating yourself up over it. Instead, use that energy to develop your coping strategies. By being committed to change and keeping yourself fit and healthy you will be in the best possible position to tackle your phobia directly. In this chapter we look at the key factors you will need to consider if you are going to be successful in kicking those unwanted fears into touch.

For many people, their phobia or other psychological condition has such a hold over them, it becomes a key part of their identity. They start to use labels such as 'I am a depressive', 'I am an alcoholic' and 'I am an anorexic'. However, these labels (which are referred to as 'master labels', as they dominate and overshadow all other characteristics) can be less than helpful. You may be someone who suffers from one or more of these conditions, but they do not define who you are. Using labels like these denies the complexity and richness of your whole personal identity. In addition, you are actually inflating the power of your problem and wasting considerable energy as a consequence.

You are More than Your Fear

I want you to consider your phobia or fears about flying as a separate entity from yourself. Picture it as the imp described in Chapter 10. This imp is just an interloper who is living aspects of your life. He is not *you* and is no more than a parasite or bully who should be sent packing.

By looking to adopt a positive and determined approach to learning how to fly with confidence, you will be putting your imp on notice that the status quo will be changing.

Offer Yourself Encouragement and Respect

It is important to recognise the importance of conserving your energy to constructively deal with the problem, rather than wasting it beating yourself up. You shouldn't consider yourself a failure or a coward for being unable to fly comfortably. After all, you didn't wish your difficulty with flying on yourself any more than someone would have wished on themselves to become physically ill. Just as a person with diabetes has to learn how to manage their physical condition, so too you need to learn how to manage your psychological condition.

Most people will instinctively encourage others who are struggling with a problem. However, for some extraordinary reason, we don't give the same standards of respect and support to ourselves. Instead, we tend to berate ourselves and belittle our attempts if we are not instantly successful in effecting change. You would never dream of treating a child, friend or colleague in this manner, so why do it to yourself?

I want you to learn to be your own best friend and supporter, offering yourself unconditional positive regard and respect. This will help you increase your self-confidence as you work towards resolving your problem.

Never Give in to Bullies

Returning to the imp (your phobia), I have no doubt that many of you, over time, have done your best to appease and placate this bully. Frequently, I have asked nervous flyers on board a flight, 'How are you feeling?' to get the response, 'Fine for the moment but I am not sure how long it can last!' At the time, the person felt fully in control but wasn't confident this feeling was going to continue. They didn't want to appear too cocky just in case their imp wreaked revenge on them for their display of confidence. Even if the imp did have this power, which it does not, the psychology is totally wrong as the more we concede to a bully the more powerful it becomes.

From childhood we are taught that bullies gorge on our fear so we must stand up to them – your pesky imp is no exception.

Change is Challenging

As you embark upon the following chapters, I want to emphasise that effecting change is seldom a straightforward linear journey. I want you to keep this in mind as you may often take two steps forward and then one step back. Your courage and confidence may ebb and flow but your commitment to change must remain steadfast.

I value myself and will never concede defeat no matter how long it takes to achieve success.

Look After Yourself

Whenever you face a challenge in life, you are much more likely to succeed if you are taking care of yourself. By this I am referring to eating healthily, exercising regularly, making time for quality sleep and ensuring you prioritise rest and relaxation in your daily routine. Ensuring your well-being will put you in the strongest possible position to not only cope with the stresses of everyday life but give you the energy you need to face the challenge of overcoming your phobia.

In summary

In order to be able to tackle a fear of flying, along with any phobia, successfully, it's important that we are coming at it from the right place. We need to be prepared both mentally and physically by acknowledging the key factors that will help to ensure our progress. These include:

- Acceptance of the problem
- Motivation to change
- Being proactive in finding the support, skills and knowledge to make the change
- Open mindedness towards new learning
- Offering yourself respect and encouragement
- Not allowing the problem to define who you are
- Not limiting your ability to change
- Not trying to appease and placate bullies

- Accepting that change is challenging
- Never giving in to fear
- Keeping your body fit and healthy
- Keeping your mind refreshed and relaxed

> Remember that to falter is not to fail. The only failure is not to try in the first place.

Your Psychological Toolbox

Being in the right mindset for overcoming your fears is essential to your success but having psychological techniques to employ when panic and anxiety do strike is equally vital. Having a 'psychological toolbox' of these techniques at your disposal is your main weapon to help you manage your phobia. I call these techniques in your toolbox the four 'R's:

1. **REACT** – how to react
2. **REGULATE** – how to regulate breathing
3. **RELAX** – how to relax your muscles
4. **REHEARSE** – the importance of rehearsing a positive scene

These techniques will provide you with everything you need to keep your fears at bay. Further good news is the fact that they have universal application. Once learnt, they can be applied to any anxiety-provoking situation you may ever encounter throughout your entire life.

In the following chapters, I will be explaining each one of the four 'R's in depth and exactly how to utilise these tools to successfully manage your fear of flying. When these techniques are consistently applied you will have far greater control over how you choose to respond to whatever life throws at you.

Arrest your anxiety before a panic attack becomes established – prevention is better than cure.

CHAPTER 13

HOW TO REACT

Nothing diminishes anxiety faster than action.

Walter Anderson

would like to introduce you to the first 'R' of your 'psychological toolbox', which will enable you to manage acute anxiety/panic. The first 'R' stands for *React* or, to be more explicit, react to the fact that you are experiencing anxiety symptoms.

Learn to read the warning signs

We all know when we are not feeling comfortable. But how do we know this? Quite simply from the sensations and feelings we experience from our body and mind. For some, it is the fact that they start to disengage from what is happening around them and they find it difficult to respond to normal interaction and communication. Some report that everything starts to feel surreal. Others manifest their discomfort on a physical or visceral level, experiencing perhaps a headache, sweaty palms, dry throat or a nervous tummy.

It is crucial for your own well-being that you learn to read the signs of your phobia and then react to the situation at the earliest stage. Sadly, my experience has taught me that people waste valuable energy either just wishing the symptoms away or desperately trying to conceal them so as not to alert those around them that they are struggling. Both of these actions are futile and are a waste of valuable resources. By prioritising your ability to react constructively to the situation you can save yourself from an inordinate amount of unnecessary discomfort and distress. It is all about taking that first step of reacting. This chapter will help you acquaint yourself with the major symptoms of a phobia, so you know what to look out for when they do occur so that you can try to *react* as early as possible.

What is happening to me?

THE PANIC ATTACK

Does the following scenario sound familiar?

The holiday has been finalised and booked. Everyone concerned is basking in anticipatory excitement, longingly awaiting the start of the vacation. That is, everyone but you! From the moment the credit card details were exchanged with the travel company a sense of cold dread pervaded your life. The finality of the booking confirmation heralded the commencement of the excruciatingly relentless countdown to your forthcoming ordeal. You know that you are in for a regime of sleepless nights, comfort eating and hideous irritability. Family and friends give you a wide berth, apart from kindly acknowledging that you look tired and really must be looking forward to your holiday! 'Don't worry,' they reassure you, 'it won't be long before you are on the aircraft and can kick back, relax and recharge your batteries.' The only kicking back you want to do is using the well-wisher's backside as a target as their benevolently intended comments further fuel your terror. You mentally rehearse in minute detail how you will lose the plot, embarrass yourself and mortify those accompanying you. As the date of departure draws ever nigh, your anticipatory anxiety inexorably builds to a crescendo. This relentless build-up will then undoubt-edly climax in your total meltdown at the airport in full public view on the allotted departure date. You know that it is inevitable that you will single-handedly completely wreck the holiday for your entire party and most probably will have to be restrained in a straitjacket by mental health offi-cials as your critical faculties proceed to go AWOL at the airport. This naturally will culminate in the flight being delayed, much to the chagrin and dismay of your travelling companions who are gallantly holding back the baying mob of homicidal fellow passengers whose flight connections have been screwed up by your selfish antics. All of this shame and humiliation pales into insignificance as the over-whelming panic attack finds you imploring your maker to dispatch you forthwith rather than endure another second of the insufferable terror you are currently experiencing. Death would indeed be a relief!

Okay, perhaps the previous description is a touch over the top, but I am sure that reading this through you are experi-encing at least a faint resonance with the above scenario!

ACUTE ANXIETY OR A PANIC ATTACK?

Anxiety is the state of being uneasy and apprehensive, which simply translates into being worried. A panic attack is the body's natural reaction to the anticipation of extreme danger. It is part of our survival repertoire and involves the switching of the body from long-term survival mode to short-term emergency survival mode. Basically, this means that the body shuts down any unnecessary processes and directs its entire capacity to ensuring survival in that moment. This process is brought about by the activation of the fight-or-flight response, which is the release of stress hormones into the bloodstream (see Chapter 11, page 114). This engenders instant changes in our respiratory, circulatory and digestive systems, which can be very distressing.

Am I losing my mind?

I always try to reassure people who, as a result of experiencing anxiety/panic attacks, fear that they are losing their mind, as follows: firstly, it would be a pretty hopeless survival mechanism if it induced dementia, which would seriously compromise the likelihood of our long-term survival. Secondly, anyone who is worried that they are losing their mind has, de facto, not done so. Someone who has lost their mind does not have the mental capacity to consider this possibility, or they wouldn't care anyway.

Why does my tummy feel so uncomfortable?

In short-term emergency survival mode, our digestive system suddenly shuts down and many of us experience phenomena ranging from the mild sense of butterflies in our tummy to diarrhoea and nausea. The latter symptoms have a three-fold survival quality in that by halting the digestive process, spare capacity is made available since the blood vessels in the digestive tract constrict and blood is pumped at a faster rate to the major muscles to enable us to run away or fight. Secondly, by vomiting or evacuating our bowels (or, heaven forbid, both!), we become lighter and therefore technically can run away faster from the threat. Finally, if we are captured by the threat, we will not smell too appetising and therefore have a faint chance of not being gobbled up (similar to skunks who emit a noxious odour to dissuade would-be attackers) as the predator may well spy another unsuspecting victim while temporarily holding its nose while it summons up the courage to dine!

Why do I sweat and have eyes like saucers?

Symptoms of a panic attack are based on survival qualities, such as the dilation of your eyes to let in more light and information. Sweating is also a response to our emotional state of being frightened. Our fearful state causes an increase in the activity of the sympathetic nervous system. This state of arousal leads to increased muscle activity in preparation for the fight-or-flight response and generates an increase in your body temperature. Sweating is the body's mechanism for getting rid of excess heat, caused by the increased metabolic activity.

I could wax lyrical about a plethora of symptoms, but my intention is to offer a general overview of what is actually happening to you when you experience acute anxiety/panic. What is most important is for you to learn to recognise *your* symptoms of distress at the earliest opportunity, be they chest pains or shaking, increased irritability or an inability to focus and concentrate. Even frequent yawning can be an indication of your increasing level of anxiety rather than it being interpreted as just a reflection of tiredness.

> Everyone's symptoms are different. Learn to identify yours at their inception so that you can *react* immediately.

WHY IS HAVING A PANIC ATTACK SO UNBEARABLE?

Over the years many clients have articulated that acute anxiety, leading to a full-blown panic attack, is the worst experience that they have ever endured in their life.

The reason that this experience is so overwhelmingly uncomfortable (uncomfortable! now that is an understatement if ever I heard one!) is because it is a process that is trying to alert you to the fact that your very survival is in jeopardy so you must react immediately. The more intense the warning signals the less chance of them being ignored. To convey the urgency of the message in the most effective way the 'General' (the amygdala, see Chapter 11, page 114) leaves nothing to chance. He instantly sends a message, which results in the adrenal glands deploying a cocktail of stress hormones. These in turn cause a powerful impact on the following four domains:

1. Psychological – this encompasses our cognitions/thoughts
2. Emotional – our feelings, moods
3. Behavioural – how we act, e.g. avoidance
4. Physiological – bodily/somatic responses, physical symptoms

As we can see from the list above, to be caught in the throes of acute anxiety that then develops into a full-blown panic attack is debilitating to say the least. It is all encompassing and there is no quarter in which to hide, no area of respite as both your mind and body are totally involved in the process.

Let us look at these domains in greater detail, starting with the psychological category. These are just some of the symptoms, which may be experienced, and it is important that you learn to recognise them in order to arrest the panic at the earliest possible stage.

Recognise the symptoms and then you can react

1. Psychological symptoms

Fear of losing control
A sense of impending doom or dread
Intense difficulty in concentrating
Short-term memory loss
Being easily distracted

Preoccupation with health concerns
Confusion
Inability to control thinking
Fear of being rejected
Fear of losing consciousness
Fear of going mad
Fear of dying
Déjà vu
Fear of what people think of you
Feeling strange or odd
Loss of confidence
Low self-esteem
Feeling insecure

2. Emotional symptoms

Fearful
Terrified
Irritable
Depressed
Sad
Guilty
Edgy
Uneasy
Jittery
Impatient
Wound up
Tense
Nervous
Anxious
Insecure
Exhausted
Angry
Useless
Worthless

Helpless
Mood swings

3. Behavioural symptoms

Avoidance
Restlessness (pacing up and down)
Postural collapse
Speech problems like stuttering
Fleeing
Hyperventilation
Feel you have to force yourself to breathe
Impaired coordination
Grinding teeth
Withdrawal from activities
Change in sleeping patterns
Jolting awake
Clenching of jaw
Nervous habits (twitching, foot tapping)
Fidgeting
Change of eating habits
Frequent yawning
Forgetfulness
Startle easily
Unsteady
Lack of focus
Cravings for sweet food substances
Repeated need to visit the loo

4. Physiological symptoms

Heart palpitations
Pounding heart
Weak muscles
Pins and needles

Numbness
Shortness of breath
Hot and cold spells
Nausea
Abdominal pain
Tremors, trembling and shaking
Sweating
Dizziness, giddiness, floating sensations
Diarrhoea
Aches and pains
Tense muscles
Indigestion
Burning sensations on skin
Chest tightness
Lack of energy
Feeling weak
Headaches
Sensitive eyes

Avoiding the situation at any cost

As you can see from the above lists, it is not surprising that people will go to great lengths to avoid the situations which bring on these symptoms. Avoidance is, in fact, one of the defining characteristics of a phobia. Later in the book we will explore how we can prevent this intense state of discomfort. Once you are armed with your four 'R's toolbox, you will be equipped to bring these domains back under control.

Vicious cycle

If the symptoms described above were not bad enough, your imagination conspires to make the situation even worse. It further fuels the terror, by adding fears concerning the symptoms experienced, thus inducing a vicious cycle. Our 'imps' (phobias) never knowingly miss out on an opportunity for further sport and will convince us that we have the medical or psychiatric expertise to form diagnoses, deduced from the symptoms displayed.

Take a look at the following examples and perhaps you might even recognise your own experience from a previous flight.

Perpetuation of panic

Symptoms	Thoughts and worries
Acute chest pains	'I am going to suffer a heart attack and die'
Uncomfortable cognitive changes	'I am losing my mind and going mad'
Difficulty in breathing	'This will cause apnoea and then death'
Feeling faint	'I am going to fall into a coma and then die'

I often discuss these scenarios with nervous flyers and they are always accompanied by a great deal of laughter as people recognise their behaviour. This is good for two reasons: firstly it normalises the behaviour, as people often feel ashamed and embarrassed that they have over-reacted in this way and frequently feel that they are the only ones that imagine such dire consequences. Then, by laughing at themselves they both diminish the power of the phobia along with releasing endorphins, which are the body's natural antidote to stress. Laughter is, in fact, the best tonic that you can give to yourself.

Laughter relaxes. And relaxation is spiritual.
Bhagwan Shree Rajineesh

> **Failure to deal with the perceived threat through fight or flight causes our body to be flooded with stress hormones.**

Those of you who have been fortunate enough never to have experienced anxiety and panic to this level might well think that the above scenarios are a gross exaggeration. I would like to assure you that, sadly, this is far from the case. What is actually happening is that the General (amygdala) becomes increasingly alarmed by the frightening and unusual symptoms and therefore calls for an escalation of reinforcements to meet the threat. In short, he sends in more Cavalry (stress hormones). This further deluge of stress hormones into the system serves to amplify the symptoms to an unbearable level. As they are not deployed to serve the purpose for which they were designed, that is, 'fight or flee', they continue to build up. In effect, this is experienced by the body as an internal insurrection, that is, an attack upon itself.

It is rather like crying wolf, in that the Cavalry, which has been urgently called in, is not put to use and, irritated by the false alarm, makes itself an uncomfortable guest in our body. The good news is that the body is designed to withstand this level of panic so, although extremely distressing for the sufferer, it is not in fact dangerous.

Take charge of the situation

It is important to realise that *you* are the author of your own suffering. Allowing high levels of anxiety to go unchecked in this manner could well result in a panic attack. The panic attack will then produce frightening symptoms, which in turn will be assessed by the amygdala as dangerous and threatening. This will result in the release of even more stress hormones, causing a repeat of the vicious cycle, which is now in place, thus perpetuating the panic attack. To put it another way, you are freaking yourself out.

Remember that 'knowledge is power', and to know that you are the driver in creating your own agony puts you in a powerful position. You are no longer the loyal subject of your 'imp' but a mover and a shaker, who can bring about your own salvation, quite simply by *reacting*!

What can you do to avoid this vicious cycle or at least halt it once it has begun?

This is where you apply your first 'R' – React. By reacting to the fact that you are becoming distressed, you will immediately let your imp (phobia) know that you are on to him and do not intend to allow him to call the shots. Obviously, the earlier you intervene, the easier it is to achieve this, since at the earlier stage you still have access to your decision-making part of the brain, the 'Sovereign' (the neocortex).

As you are now aware, once the threat reaches a certain level, the seat of government relocates from the 'Sovereign' to the 'General' (amygdala) and emergency protocol ensues. Speaking biologically, the amygdala takes command and you switch over from long-term survival mode and conscious control to short-term emergency survival mode and unconscious control.

THE BEST WAY TO REACT IS TO DISTRACT

The following exercise perfectly demonstrates how the simplest and most effective way of reacting to anxiety symptoms is to offer some form of distraction.

1. Place a rubber band on your wrist and twang it sufficiently so that it hurts.
2. Yell to yourself '*Stop!*'
3. Apply a positive statement/affirmation such as: '*I am in control and will choose how I live my life.*'

Let us explore the above further. All three actions in combination help us achieve the desired result – breaking the vicious circle of anxiety and panic. The sole purpose of the rubber band is merely to distract our attention away from the subversive injunctions of our 'imp' or phobia that, if given free rein, will fill our mind with all manner of terrors. It will pose as our ally and friend, imploring us to save our soul by withdrawing from the situation: our intention to take a flight. The phobia will promote avoidance in a most compelling fashion and without a previously thought-out strategy is more than likely to triumph and get its way. The experience of the pain shocks us into action, so that we consciously cry out 'enough is enough'. Our rational mind wants to be free to travel at will. This is then followed up by a positive statement that confirms that we are back in charge of things.

To react enables us to take back control to follow our original course of action, i.e. to follow the travel plans you have made, rather than be incapacitated by the phobia's grasp. This strategy works by momentarily, at the point when the rubber band is twanged, enabling us to refocus our mind. In this case, it is quite simply that as a result of this action, we are forced to acknowledge pain. When we experience pain we instantly banish other preoccupations, which have been highlighted by our 'imp'. These thoughts may have ranged from 'this is going to be a very uncomfortable flight' through to 'your very existence is in the balance'. Regardless of the intensity of the thought, the snapping of your rubber band instantly arrests the thought and enables you (the Sovereign) to regain ascendency.

In other words, the firing up of your pain receptors wipes clear the messages promulgated by the phobia and gives you time to seize the initiative. You are now in a position to select your chosen course of action.

On our Flying with Confidence course, we frequently encourage clients to practise this technique in relation to the prospect of turbulence. As mentioned in Chapter 4 (page 44), turbulence may be uncomfortable but it is not dangerous. So an appropriate positive statement in this context might be as follows:

'I can cope with turbulence. This is not a safety issue. It merely makes me feel uncomfortable.'

It is wise to be mindful of Epictetus, a Greek Stoic philosopher who noted the following observation: *'The thing that upsets people is not what happens but what they think it means.'*

Let us look closer at this phenomenon known as turbulence. You and I experience the same objective reality and yet we both interpret it differently. For me, it is quite simply a change in the flow of air movement, somewhat akin to the variations experienced on a calm or rough sea. If I am absolutely honest, I actually enjoy turbulence since I find that it serves to break up the monotony of a long journey. If it is very mild, it makes me feel soporific and rocks me off to sleep. If the turbulence is more energetic, then I enjoy the movement in the same way that I relish fairground rides.

However, many people with a fear of flying are struck with abject terror when confronted with turbulence on an aeroplane, and interpret it as a life-and-death situation.

> *If you are distressed by anything external, the pain is not due to the thing itself, but to your estimate of it, and this you have the power to revoke at any moment.*
>
> Marcus Aurelius

For pilots, turbulence is a normal part of flying and is not to be feared. It might well be helpful here to turn back to Chapter 4 for a detailed explanation from Steve on this totally natural phenomenon in relation to flying and why it presents no danger. As Steve points out, pilots do recognise that turbulence distresses some passengers and interferes with the smooth running of the cabin service and therefore will try their best to avoid it whenever possible.

Superstitions and obsessive behaviour only help fuel a phobia

Sadly, one of the common features that has a tendency to emerge when people are in the grip of a phobia is that they become highly superstitious and sometimes obsessive. This disposition can start off innocuously enough in childhood. Many children try to avoid treading on the cracks of paving stones and salute a solitary magpie to ward off bad luck. Similarly, when someone is feeling anxious and vulnerable they reason that there is no point in taking any unnecessary risks and so will continue to entertain the superstition just in case there is some truth in it.

Added to the vague belief that these obtuse behaviours may offer deliverance from danger we have a further component added to the mix. This is the unwitting use of pattern matching by the 'General' (amygdala) in a futile attempt to control the environment and hence safety via ludicrous means.

What I mean by this is that people will try to replicate the exact same circumstances surrounding a previous successful flight in the misguided belief that this will be instrumental in ensuring their safety. This is executed down to the minutest detail, including choosing a flight at the same time of day that they previously flew and getting the same taxi driver to drop them off at the airport. They may wear the same travelling clothes, pack their cases in a precise manner, be allocated the same seat number, fly with the same airline and aircraft type, to mention but a few of these idiosyncrasies. We box ourselves in by unreasonably trying to control our environment. Another example of this is by interpreting the current weather conditions. If it is raining, for example, then it is an irrefutable signal that one shouldn't fly! People also attribute all sorts of predictive powers based on the state of the car park when they arrive on the course. If it was difficult to park then this is another sign that they shouldn't fly. Conversely, if parking and weather conditions are excellent then this too is a signal that they should not fly as there is clearly a conspiracy going on, with the malevolent intention of lulling them into a false sense of security! I think that you will have got the message that when all of this irrational thought is taking place, the 'imp' is very much in command.

Over the years, I have also witnessed many people arrive on the course festooned in a variety of lucky charms. They hand over their welfare to miscellaneous talismans, such as horseshoes, St Christopher medals, four-leafed clovers and a wide range of gemstones. All of these ornaments, in the eyes of the wearer, purportedly serve the function of keeping them safe from harm. If any of these devices are left behind by mistake on the day of the flight, then it is perceived as an omen that they must not fly that day. If I challenge anyone about the notion that the flight will only be safe if they and their lucky horseshoe are on board and that the pilot's training and skills are merely incidental to the enterprise, they tend to look somewhat sheepish. Nonetheless, although recognising their own gullibility, it is clear that they still would not wish to take the risk of travelling without them! But can you honestly say the wearing of your lucky underpants has a significant bearing on the safety of a forthcoming flight? It's a totally irrational notion and it's important to relinquish such rituals and superstitions, as these only serve to keep you trapped and the phobia alive.

On one occasion, I was asked by a young woman to destroy a suede pouch containing a number of charms and religious medals that were threaded on to exquisite gold chains. These had been presented to her by well-wishers to act as a form of talisman. She recognised that by attributing an almost magical power to these objects, she had, in fact, diminished her own sense of agency. For several years, this young woman, who had also suffered from agoraphobia, had not been able to venture anywhere without taking these items with her. I was reluctant to agree to destruction of the jewellery, not least because of its clear sentimental and monetary value, so I suggested reaching a compromise in that I would take temporary custody of the jewellery for one year. My reasoning was that this would give the young lady ample time to prove to herself that she could live her life independently without the need for these items. Once the year expired, the pouch was duly restored to its owner. She was then able to enjoy the jewellery for what it was: a collection of beautiful personal adornments bestowed on her by loving friends and family members, nothing more and nothing less.

Case history

Benedict acquired a fear of flying after an acrimonious divorce from his wife. The separation caused a negative impact on the couple's finances, resulting in Benedict having to work overtime to cover the increased expenses. As well as the loss of the family home, which had to be sold to finance two smaller properties, Benedict missed the regular daily contact with his two young children. Benedict's life revolved around work and visiting his children whenever he could. There was no time for friends or the pursuit of interests he had previously enjoyed. During this time, Benedict lost his appetite while, at the same time, he increased his consumption of alcohol. He found that drinking helped him to get off to sleep more easily; however, within hours, he would be wide awake worrying about his problems throughout the rest of the night.

The following day he would drink copious cups of coffee to help him to stay awake at work. He then would return home at the end of the day feeling empty and exhausted. As this cycle continued, Benedict lost weight and started to suffer from severe migraines. Eventually, he sought help from his doctor and, after visiting his GP, Benedict was signed off work and told to get some rest. Benedict's widowed mother lived in Dublin and so he decided to stay with her for a few weeks. On the flight out to Dublin, Benedict experienced a panic attack in which he felt that he was suffocating and incapable of getting enough air into his lungs. Needless to say, at the end of his two-week visit, he cancelled his flight home and returned to England by boat.

Benedict avoided flying from this point but heeded the doctor's advice to look after his health by eating properly and reducing his alcohol intake. Benedict slowly adjusted to the situation and started to feel much more optimistic about life. Both Benedict and his ex-wife met new partners and, for several years, Benedict was able to have his children stay with him twice a week and every other weekend. During this time, Benedict still refused to fly despite encouragement from his new partner. It was not until his ex-wife announced that she was moving with her new partner to Germany that he felt compelled to address his fear of flying. Naturally, Benedict was devastated by the news that his children would be living abroad but this proved to be the catalyst that motivated him to conquer his fear of flying.

When it came time to finally facing his fear and getting on an aeroplane once more, Benedict almost turned back but he was very glad he didn't. Although it was both emotional and exhausting, since the memory of his previous panic attack was never far from his mind, Benedict was able to control his anxiety using the coping skills he had learnt and take the flight.

Benedict now flies to Germany several times per term to see his children and has totally overcome his fear of flying.

In summary

The first step to overcoming your phobia is to be able to recognise your own individual symptoms. Once you know the symptoms to look out for, you can take action. There are a range of psychological techniques, the four 'R's, at your disposal to help you manage your fear. The first is to *react* – the earlier you react to the fact that you are becoming distressed, the easier it will be to take the initiative and take control.

- React at the earliest opportunity when experiencing symptoms of distress to prevent panic from setting in.
- Twanging a rubber band on your wrist gives you a tangible signal that you intend to refocus your mind.
- Have ready a positive affirmation to replace the negative feelings of the phobia, such as: *'I can do this, I am in control.'*

Living your life in fear is not an option, since this is not living but merely existing.

CHAPTER 14

REGULATE YOUR BREATHING

Breathing is possibly the most automatic of our bodily functions, and is, of course, vital for life. It is also one of the first things to suffer whenever we feel stress or frightened. Hyperventilation, or over-breathing, is a very common symptom of a panic attack; typically, as our breathing quickens, our levels of anxiety increase. The simplest and most effective method of restoring calm and relaxing the body in any stressful situation is to slow down your breathing. Slow, rhythmic breathing is the hallmark of a relaxed, unthreatened organism or person and regulating our breathing is the second 'R' of our psychological toolkit against phobias, and it is definitely the most important of all.

If you forget everything else but the second 'R' then you are still equipped to control any anxiety/panic attack.

> Don't suffer from role confusion. Let the pilots operate the aircraft and you operate your lungs.

Relaxation through regulating breathing

If we slow down our breathing, our bodies have no option other than to relax. It is biologically impossible to have a panic attack when breathing slowly, particularly when the out-breath is longer than the in-breath, which achieves a state of relaxation more rapidly.

We cannot simultaneously be in a state of agitation while being in a state of relaxation.

By breathing slowly we can effectively mechanically override the fight-or-flight response mechanism. Even if the response is in full flow as a result of a perceived threat, causing stress hormones to be pumped through our body to prepare us to fight or flee from the danger, we can arrest the process. Obviously, it is better to intercept the response before it reaches this point, which is why you alert yourself via the first 'R' – you react to your distress at a stage that pre-empts the deployment of the stress hormones.

You may be highly sceptical that the simple act of breathing slowly can yield such powerful results. But if you look around and observe people carefully, you will notice that relaxed people do not hyperventilate.

When the breath wanders the mind also is unsteady. But when the breath is calmed the mind too will be still, and the yogi achieves long life. Therefore, one should learn to control the breath.

Svatmarama

Breathing with conscious control

Breathing is an unconscious process that happens naturally, in that we do not have to remember to breathe. However, it can be brought under conscious control. We do this happily when swimming or singing when we consciously alter our normal breathing pattern to accommodate the activity. We can also choose to do this in the face of a perceived threat that we know is irrational by electing to slow our breathing down.

It is by capitalising on this unique dual quality of both unconscious and conscious control of our breathing pattern that we can induce a state of calmness and relaxation. This will open up the route to the thinking part of the brain, thus gaining us access to the neocortex. By gaining access we will not only experience a sense of personal control, but it will also diminish the terrifying feeling of losing one's mind.

Why our breathing pattern changes in the presence of threat

As I have already mentioned, the fight-or-flight response activates our short-term emergency survival mode, which brings the body to a state of preparedness to handle the perceived threat. If we are to fight or escape, we need our bodies to be at their strongest and fastest to deal with the danger. To achieve this heightened state of powerfulness the body needs to take in greater quantities of oxygen.

Oxygen is essential for the creation of energy. When we are in fight-or-flight mode, the demand for energy is amplified enormously compared to when our body is at rest. The oxygen enters the bloodstream from the lungs and is distributed throughout the body. The muscles and tissue absorb the oxygen and this, along with glucose, enables the body to produce the energy it requires. As a by-product of this activity, carbon dioxide is produced and this is eliminated from the body by being carried by the bloodstream back to the lungs where it is exhaled.

The body achieves this by automatically speeding up our breathing from slow, relaxed, deep abdominal breathing to rapid, shallow, thoracic breathing to increase the oxygen intake. This is a perfectly normal and helpful response for a short-term emergency and once the threat has subsided the body should return to the status quo, that is, slow, deep abdominal breathing.

Habitual shallow breathing

But here is the rub. Many of us persist with entertaining a constant low level of anxiety, having developed a state of 'learnt perpetual worrying'. As a consequence, we have formed the habit of shallow breathing. Although we may not be hyperventilating in the true sense of the term, we continue to breathe using only the upper part of the body, ingesting air as far as the ribcage, but not reaching as far as the diaphragm, which lies beneath the ribcage.

As a consequence of this type of breathing we are sending a message to the brain or, to be precise, to our General (the amygdala), that the threat has not totally dissipated and therefore the state of hyper-vigilance and preparedness must endure. As previously explained, this causes a vicious cycle to be set up whereby the brain is in a semi-permanent defensive mode and interprets innocuous incoming data as threatening, purely by virtue of this hyper-alert state.

To understand this phenomenon the following analogy may be helpful. Imagine the conscientious vigilance of a distressed parent after witnessing their young child suffer a life-threatening illness. Long after the child's recovery, the anxious parent continues to stress over the most marginal rise in the child's temperature. Normal changes will be misconstrued as having the most negative interpretations. This is because the parent is primed and alert to danger as a result of their recent harrowing experience.

Correct breathing

We are born with a natural capacity to enjoy the state of being relaxed, as evidenced by the way small babies breathe slowly and contentedly when warm and dry and after being fed. However, as life takes its toll, we lose this skill in a misguided attempt to control our environment from all potential threat. Paradoxically, it is by taking this unrealistic stance that we inadvertently place ourselves in a less resourceful position. Constant worrying not only ruins the quality of our lives psychologically, but also plays a part in disrupting our sleep patterns, which causes a knock-on effect physiologically, not least to the healthiness of our immune system. The good news is that the more we practise relaxation the more we inhibit the release of stress hormones as our tolerance level increases.

Correct breathing can easily be achieved with persistent practice. As it is a skill we all possessed in abundance as infants, we are not learning something new but merely resurrecting something that we have inadvertently distorted. In effect, we need to rectify bad habits that we have acquired over the years.

You cannot always control what goes on outside. But you can always control what goes on inside.

Wayne Dyer

Techniques for breathing correctly

The following breathing techniques will help you learn how to prevent agitation or reverse the consequences of the fight-or-flight response if it has already been triggered. If you are a singer or do meditation, yoga or Pilates then you are probably familiar with these techniques already. It is important to learn the most simplified set of techniques, since anticipatory anxiety inhibits our ability to use the neocortex. What follows can, therefore, be employed even by people in a heightened state of distress as well as by those who wish to use it for prevention purposes.

Follow your natural breathing pattern

I would like to point out that some people can become very anxious about not doing the techniques correctly. The bottom line is that we are trying to achieve, as a minimum, your natural breathing pattern and this is *good enough*.

Whether you breathe in or out through the nose or mouth or a combination of both is not particularly relevant. What is important is to pursue a manner of breathing that feels the most comfortable or natural for you. Some people suffer from a variety of nasal problems and prefer to breathe in and out through the mouth. This is absolutely fine.

Develop the style that suits you best. Technically speaking, it is considered better to breathe in and out through the nose on account of the aperture being smaller than the mouth and hence this automatically helps to slow things down. It is far easier to gulp air down quickly via the mouth than to rapidly snort it up through the nose. I personally prefer the in-breath to be taken through the nose and the out-breath through the mouth as this creates a smooth continuous circular motion, which I find more relaxing and soporific.

EXERCISE 1: 4/4 BASIC BREATHING TECHNIQUE

To avoid adding to any anticipatory anxiety you may already be feeling, I want to start off as simply as possible, just aiming to slow the breathing pace down. I have found over the years that, once people experience the instant benefits of 4/4 breathing, they are more than willing to invest in the heightened rewards of differentiated breathing, that is, the extended out-breath in relation to the in-breath.

1. Sit comfortably and place one hand on your upper chest (your thumb and forefinger forming a V at the base of your neck) and your other hand on your abdomen (roughly between your belt and belly button – see box opposite on belly breathing).
2. Exhale breath. An effective way to do this is to sigh as if exhausted. This will not only ensure that you have expelled the air from your lungs but will also make you relax your shoulders and allow them to sink down rather than pulling them up tensely towards your ears.
3. To the count of four inhale air by pushing your stomach out so it is distended (rather like inflating a set of bellows or a balloon). Your hand, placed on your abdomen should move significantly outwards. Try to avoid pulling your shoulders up as 'up and down' breathing is wrong and 'out and in' breathing is correct. You will know if you are doing this correctly as the hand on your upper chest should be moving significantly less than the hand placed on your abdomen. At the same time, silently say to yourself the word 'calm'.
4. Exhale breath to the count of four by pulling your stomach in which will enable the air to be expelled, leaving your stomach as flat as possible. This time, the hand placed on your abdomen should move significantly

inwards as you tense your stomach muscles. Check that the hand on your chest is scarcely moving or moving significantly less than the hand placed on your abdomen: as in the inhale breath, 'up and down' breathing is wrong and 'out and in' breathing is correct. At the same time silently say the word '*relax*'.

5. Repeat steps 3 and 4 until you start to feel calm and the physical symptoms of anxiety begin to abate. Once you are confident that you are breathing correctly then you will no longer need to place your hands on your chest and abdomen.

Belly breathing

The reason why I advocate that one hand is placed on the abdomen and the other on the chest is to help to ensure that breathing is done correctly. We are aiming for deep diaphragmatic breathing, also known as 'belly breathing', as opposed to shallow thoracic breathing. The diaphragm is the large muscle that extends horizontally, separating the chest cavity (which accommodates the heart and lungs) from the stomach cavity. It is located directly below the ribcage.

When we breathe in deeply, the diaphragm contracts and pushes down into the abdomen, thereby enlarging the volume capacity of the thoracic cavity. At the same time, the abdomen expands, causing our stomach to distend. As well as enhancing the available volume, the contraction of the muscle causes a suction effect, which helps to draw air down into the tiny alveoli, grape-like structures in the lungs. It is at the site of each tiny alveolus that the gas exchange takes place, enabling oxygen to be absorbed into the blood in exchange for carbon dioxide, which is then released from the lungs during exhalation. As we breathe out, the process is reversed as the relaxed diaphragm springs back to its original position, just below the ribcage, facilitating the expulsion of the exhaled air.

If you have any uncertainty about how to breathe correctly, try watching a baby breathing when they are asleep as they demonstrate the perfect breathing technique. You will see that they naturally use their tummy to perform 'out and in' breathing, a far cry from the erroneous 'up and down' breathing acquired by many adults.

Lung visualisation

Try to visualise your lungs, each of which is made up of approximately 350 million tiny alveoli (air sacs). Picture this grape-like structure turning blue as cool, calming, oxygenated air is inhaled and then see the structure turn pink as the gas exchange has taken place, enabling the carbon dioxide-enriched air to be expelled from the body during exhalation. Along with the carbon dioxide being expelled, visualise all your worries and fears being released from your body at the same time.

By imagining what is taking place in our lungs, we mentally assist the relaxation process and distract ourselves from following any negative line of thought, which only serves to keep the anxiety alive. This is how the 'Sovereign' (the neocortex) takes command by sending positive mental images to the 'General' (the amygdala), while also ensuring at the same time that the pesky 'imp' doesn't get a look in.

EXERCISE 2: SOOTHING WORDS VISUALISATION

Another technique is to visualise, with eyes closed, the words *'calm'* and *'relax'* in conjunction with the in- and out-breath respectively. Imagine these words in lower case, then upper case, italics, a combination of lower and upper case, and every variety of colours. This too keeps the brain occupied and denies the phobia the opportunity to sew further negative thoughts.

EXERCISE 3: 7/11 BREATHING TECHNIQUE

This is the acknowledged crème de la crème of breathing techniques and one that can be extremely beneficial. For this technique, the out-breath is considerably longer than the in-breath, which automatically forces the body to rapidly succumb to the relaxation mode, having stimulated the para-sympathetic nervous system. This technique requires considerable practice but fully repays the effort. It is helpful to initially practise this technique while lying on the floor with a book placed on your stomach. This way it is easier to monitor that the entire abdomen is being used since the inhalation, if done properly, will cause the diaphragm to push down into the abdominal cavity causing the book to rise. As the air is slowly expelled, the book will gently fall back to its original position.

1. Expel air
2. Slowly and steadily inhale air to the count of 7
3. Slowly and steadily exhale air to the count of 11. If you struggle with this then simply wait up until the count of 11 before inhaling again
4. Repeat steps 2 and 3 for 5 to 10 minutes

This is an excellent exercise to do whenever the opportunity presents itself, such as waiting in a queue or traffic jam.

Those of you who are adept at multi-tasking can tie it in with doing pelvic-floor exercises at the same time!

EXERCISE 4: THE BROWN PAPER BAG TECHNIQUE

The brown paper bag technique (or the 'sick bag' technique) is far and away the most conspicuous and un-glamorous of breathing techniques but wonderfully effective. If you feel so agitated that counting and controlling your breathing seems impossible due to the adverse effects of too much adrenalin, then this is the technique for you.

When you hyperventilate you take in too much oxygen. Your body needs a certain amount of carbon dioxide to extract the oxygen from your blood but when you over-breathe you do not give your body long enough to retain the carbon dioxide and so your body cannot use the oxygen you have. This technique is highly successful because it involves re-inhaling the breath you just exhaled, which is replete with carbon dioxide. The brown paper bag technique is just a short-term emergency method when the sufferer is so out of control that they are unable to do 4/4 breathing/measured breathing techniques.

Please note that you should always use this method with a degree of caution, as excessive use of this technique may cause the reverse problem, a deficit of oxygen, which will result in light-headedness.

1. Place a paper bag around your mouth and nose ensuring that it is sealed as completely as possible to ensure that no air can escape.
2. Breathe in and out until the negative symptoms of the stress hormones abate and you feel able to control your breathing. This will vary from individual to individual depending on your metabolism and degree of agitation. Take about six breaths, check how you feel and if the

symptoms persist, take another six breaths and continue like this. As soon as you feel sufficiently in control to remove the paper bag and return to the controlled breathing of in for four and out for four, do so as this is by far the most effective way to reduce panic.

Case history

Ellen's mother and two younger brothers had emigrated to Mexico 12 years ago. Each year since, Ellen had visited her mother to spend Christmas with her and the siblings. Three years ago Ellen married James and soon after the couple's son Cameron was born. Cameron, who was not quite a year old, was to spend time with his paternal grandmother while Ellen and James made their annual trip to Mexico.

Shortly after boarding the aeroplane, Ellen started to hyperventilate and shake uncontrollably. James, a paramedic, tried to reassure her that this was a panic attack, which would pass if she slowed down her breathing. Despite James's reassurances, Ellen was convinced that she was about to have a heart attack and insisted on getting off the aircraft. The couple returned home and Ellen was horrified by her reaction. On top of the terror, which she had experienced during the panic attack, she felt guilty about the disappointment that she had caused her mother, partner and siblings. Ellen avoided flights from that point until she received an invitation to the marriage of her youngest brother. Recognising that her fear of flying was seriously compromising her freedom to join this important family celebration, Ellen sought help by attending a course. I am delighted to say that Ellen did fly to Mexico for her brother's wedding and young Cameron met his maternal grandmother for the first time.

In summary

It is biologically impossible to be in a state of agitation while simultaneously being in a state of relaxation. By slowing down your breathing and prolonging your out-breath, you engage the parasympathetic nervous system in producing this relaxed mode. The second 'R', *regulate*, takes in the following:

- Focus on your breathing immediately after twanging the rubber band and expressing a positive affirmation.
- Sit comfortably and exhale the air from your body.
- To the count of four, inhale air, saying the word '*calm*' silently to yourself.
- To the count of four, exhale air, saying the word '*relax*' silently to yourself.
- Repeat the previous two steps until your breathing is brought under control.

By achieving mastery over our breathing, we gain mastery over how we live our life. The converse is also true since a peaceful mind will result in an easy breath.

CHAPTER 15

RELAX YOUR MUSCLES

Your mind and your body are inextricably bound together. Their mutual influence is such that a tense mind causes a tense body and a tense body causes a tense mind.

Now is the time to introduce you to the third 'R' in your psychological toolbox – *relax*. Or to be more precise – relax your muscles. Just as the mind needs to be calm and stable, so too the body needs to be free from serious tension in order to send out the right signals that there is no imminent threat or danger. If our muscles are tense, the feedback loop to the brain registers this as the organism being at risk or in crisis. And, yes, it will result in exactly the same reaction as rapid breathing causes, that is, the body will be flooded with a cocktail of stress hormones to combat the perceived threat. As we now know, this is the last thing we want when our fear has triggered a false emergency situation as the side effects of the stress hormones not only maintain the panic but exacerbate the situation.

Just as it was imperative to halt the hyperventilation discussed in the previous chapter, you now must focus on reducing the tension in your body.

Many of you will already be acutely aware of the areas in your body in which tension tends to collect. It may be in the muscles within the shoulder area, the jaw or the neck, to name but a few popular sites for severe muscle tension. For others, the back area, particularly the lower back, is more susceptible. This, of course, accounts for the large percentage of people suffering from back complaints for which no organic cause can be discerned.

The increased muscle tension in the larger muscles plays a key role in the short-term survival mode, as these are the muscles that will be used in fight or flight. Equally, the tensing of the jaw and shoulders acts to present a threatening stance towards an aggressor. This is intended to intimidate the predator in the hope that it will back off and discontinue the attack. This is most helpful and constructive if a real physical threat exists, say if one was about to be mugged. However, if this aspect of our survival repertoire is not put to use, it merely causes acute discomfort. An uncomfortable body results in an uncomfortable mind, further fuelling the emotional anguish of an anxiety/panic attack. The mind and the body impact upon one another and each influences the other.

A cheerful frame of mind, reinforced by relaxation, is the best medicine that puts all ghosts of fear on the run.

George Matthew Adams

From a biological point of view, what is happening is that the blood, which has been diverted from non-essential areas due to the constriction of blood vessels, collects in the muscles. If it remains trapped it will lead to the build-up of toxins in the muscle tissue causing discomfort and tension. The question is: how do we release this trapped blood to remove the toxins and enable fresh blood to move freely into the muscles to relax them and remove the tension?

Progressive Muscle Relaxation

Progressive Muscle Relaxation is one of the best techniques for reducing muscle tension, which in turn causes the reduction of agitation, thus enabling the body and mind to relax. These exercises basically consist of consciously tensing or tightening the muscles in an exaggerated manner, followed by releasing or letting go of the muscles. They are termed progressive because you progressively work through the muscle groups starting from the top of the head down to the tips of the toes or vice versa. In effect, this mechanically pumps the blood and toxins out of the various muscle groups making the body feel relaxed and comfortable.

Progressive Muscle Relaxation is also an excellent exercise for insomnia and clients have frequently reported that they do not manage to conclude the exercise before they are fast asleep.

A programme for progressive muscle relaxation

Depending on your location, conduct these exercises with or without your eyes closed. I find the former more conducive if circumstances permit. If closing your eyes is not possible, then try to focus on a particular spot to concentrate your attention on the exercise. If you are doing these exercises in the comfort of your own home, you may prefer to conduct them lying down. If, however, you are in the office, on an aeroplane or trying to reduce tension as you wait in your car in a traffic jam, it is important to make yourself as comfortable as you can while sitting.

As in the breathing exercises, it is possible to conduct the following to a 4/4 rhythm as this keeps it simple and accessible. With practice, you may want to hold the tension for increasingly longer lengths of time so that the contrast between the tension and release feels even more profound.

Note: Repeat each step from 3 to 19 four times, before progressing to the next step. With each step, try to consciously appreciate the contrast between the intensity of the tension and the pleasure of the release when you allow the muscles to relax. Please be aware that when you let go of the tension this should be done instantaneously to feel the full benefit of the limp, relaxed muscles.

1. Find a comfortable position and focus on your breathing, ensuring that it is slow and measured.
2. Now make a conscious effort to clear your mind of worries and concerns. You can do this by repeating a meaningful mantra to yourself such as: *'I will allow myself to feel serene and calm'* or *'I experience my inner-strength and power.'*
3. Focus on your temples and scalp and tense these muscles by raising your eyebrows to the count of four and then release and relax.
4. Focus on your eyes and tense the muscles around them by screwing up your eyes, hold and then release and relax.
5. Focus on your nose and tense these muscles by furrowing your brows and flaring out your nostrils, hold and then release and relax.
6. Focus on your mouth and push your tongue against your palate, hold and then release.
7. Focus on your jaw by clenching your teeth together, hold and then release and relax.
8. Focus on your neck by turning to the left and hold for four and then to the right and hold for four. Return to the centre and relax to the count of four.
9. Focus on your shoulders and raise them up towards your ears. Hold and then release and relax.
10. Focus on your forearms by stretching your arms out in front of you while making a tight fist and squeezing. Hold and then release and relax.

11. Focus on your biceps by bending your elbows at right angles to the upper arm and tensing the muscles in your upper arm. Hold and then release and relax.
12. Focus on your hands by stretching out your arms and grasping your hands together as tightly as possible with your fingers intertwined. Hold and then release and relax.
13. Focus on your chest by drawing your shoulder blades together as close as you can. Hold and then release and relax.
14. Focus on your back by leaning your upper back and head forward forming an arc and tense your lower back. Hold and then release and relax.
15. Focus on your stomach by pushing the stomach muscles outwards making your stomach as hard as possible. Hold and then release and relax.
16. Focus on your buttocks by tensing the muscles. Hold and then release and relax.
17. Focus on your thighs by pushing your upper legs together while pushing your feet firmly into the floor. Hold and then release and relax.
18. Focus on your calves by pressing your heels into the floor while raising your toes and scrunching them up. Hold and then release and relax.
19. Focus on your feet by curling your toes down so that they make contact with the floor pushing your instep upwards into an arc. Hold and then release and relax.
20. Having worked and then relaxed all the muscles in your body, wiggle your toes and fingers and gently shrug your shoulders. Now take a few moments to allow yourself to experience the warmth, suppleness and flexibility of your relaxed body.
21. Finally, focus on your mind and notice how your cares and worries have evaporated along with the tension that was held in the body. Return to focusing on your breathing, noting how relaxed this has become. Smile and carry on with your day.

Body Audit

If you are feeling tense and do not have the luxury of time to engage in the above full Progressive Muscle Relaxation exercise, I suggest you conduct a 'body audit'. This involves swiftly scanning your body and noting the chief areas of tension. You can then target those areas where tension has collected and either select the relevant step from the Progressive Muscle Relaxation exercise or choose one of the following aircraft-friendly exercises, which most closely links to your area of tension. Having located the tense muscles, contract them to the count of four and then release to the count of four to experience the sensation of relaxation.

I will start by giving you a straightforward, general technique that can be applied to any muscle in the body to release tension. This will be followed by a series of relaxing exercises specific to different muscles and muscle groups e.g. the jaw, shoulders and neck and the chest for you to use as, and when, required.

General exercise to relax tense muscles

1. Locate the source of tension by identifying the relevant muscle.
2. Increase tension by contracting the muscle, to the count of four.
3. Release tension and relax the muscle to the count of four. You may also choose, while doing this, to silently say the word 'relax' and visualise the word or picture a relaxing scene.
4. Repeat four times.

Some of the most common areas for tension are the base and middle of the neck, shoulder (trapezius) regions, the mid-back (thoracic) region and the low back (lumbar) region. This is followed by the hands, jaws and legs.

Shoulders and neck tension release: 'the terrapin'

This action is like a tortoise retreating into its shell. It works the trapezius muscles, which are the long muscles that support the shoulders and neck. Along with the muscles at the base of the skull, they are 'stress susceptible' but are also easy to relax.

1. Sit erect.
2. Shrug your shoulders and then pull in your neck (like a tortoise going into its shell). Aim to touch your ears with your shoulders and hold the tension to the count of four.
3. To the count of four, gently rotate your head in one direction, as if trying to massage your shoulders, and then rotate in the other direction to a count of four.
4. Release the tension slowly to the count of four and let your shoulders return to their normal position. Shrug your shoulders and feel the tension drain away while silently saying *'relax'*.
5. Repeat four times to soften these muscles.

Throat tension release: 'the snob'

So called because in order to relax these muscles, which constrict when you are frightened, you need to have your nose in the air.

1. Point your chin towards the ceiling and feel the stretch in your throat.

2. Next, place your tongue on the roof of your mouth and push as hard as you can to the count of four.
3. Release the tension and lower your chin to the count of four, silently saying 'relax'.
4. Repeat four times.

Chest tension release: 'the chicken'

This unusual chicken-like action is perfect for relaxing tension in the chest.

1. Square your shoulders, with your upper and lower arms at right angles. Try not to clench your fists.
2. Try to touch your elbows behind your back.
3. Hold the tension to the count of four.
4. Release the tension to the count of four, silently saying 'relax'.
5. Repeat four times.

Diaphragm tension release: 'the boa constrictor'

Apply the squeeze like a boa constrictor to your stomach muscles to help release any tension. This is very good for dissipating light-headedness as you cannot hyperventilate while doing this exercise.

1. Sit up straight and try to pull up your stomach aiming to tuck it under your ribcage.
2. Suck in your stomach and hold to the count of four.
3. Release tension to the count of four, silently saying 'relax'. Feel the tension flow from your stomach.
4. Repeat four times.

Hands tension release: 'the hedgehog'

Anxious flyers sometimes grip the armrests of their chair and cause their hands to become extremely tense. This simple exercise, which is like a hedgehog curling and uncurling is very effective.

1. Clench both fists as tightly as you can to the count of four. Alternatively, you can grasp your hands together by intertwining your fingers and squeezing to the count of four.
2. Release the tension to the count of four, silently saying '*relax*'.
3. Repeat four times.

Jaw tension release: 'the piranha'

This is called the piranha because it looks like a fish with an underbite.

1. Extend lower jaw trying to get it beyond the teeth of the upper jaw.
2. Count to four holding the tension.
3. Release to normal position to the count of four, silently saying '*relax*'.
4. Repeat exercise four times.

Upper and lower leg tension release: 'the ballerina'

Muscle tension and hyperventilation can cause uncontrollable shaking of the legs. Try these ballerina-style stretches – perfect for releasing tightness of the leg muscles and getting rid of the shakes.

1. Sit squarely with both feet flat on the floor. Now lift one foot off the floor and point your toes towards the floor with your leg fully extended (this is for the top of your leg).
2. Hold the tension to the count of four.
3. Now pull your foot up and aim your toes towards your chin (this stretches the back of leg all the way to the buttocks).
4. Hold the tension to the count of four.
5. Allow your foot to drop to the floor and say the magic word 'relax'.
6. Repeat with the other leg.
7. Repeat both combinations four times.

Case history

I met Gilbert several years ago on one of our courses and was instantly taken with his infectious smile. I chatted to him during the lunch break and he told me that he had taken three gap years after completing his masters degree in order to travel before embarking on a PhD. The first two and a half years had been a most wonderful experience, consisting of travel in six monthly bursts interspersed with a return to the UK for three months to earn money for the next adventure. Before touring the African continent, Gilbert had been given an anti-malarial vaccine, and had an extreme adverse reaction. As a consequence, this seasoned traveller suddenly became acutely agoraphobic. For the next 18 months, Gilbert's plans had to be put on hold as he battled to retrieve his lost life. At the height of this agoraphobic episode, Gilbert was a prisoner in his own home, unable to leave his house. He also suffered from a range of physical symptoms including tinnitus, difficulty in swallowing, trembling and dizziness. With a combination of psychological help and medication, Gilbert slowly rebuilt his life. At the stage when I met him he had already conquered his fear of all other forms of travel and getting back to flying was the final frontier.

I was humbled by this courageous young man's attitude. He freely admitted that he was very scared about the forthcoming flight. He told me that no matter what it cost him, he was getting on the aircraft as he never wanted to live another moment feeling helpless under the shadow of fear. He carried no bitterness for having forfeited 18 months of his young life but said it had taught him to value every day. Words cannot describe the joy that I felt when I spoke to him after the flight. He gave me one of his engaging smiles and simply said, 'I have got my life back.'

In summary

Having a relaxed body is every bit as important as having a relaxed mind when it comes to overcoming your fear. Easing muscle tension is another way of signalling to the brain that there is no imminent threat of danger. Using the third 'R' – *relax* – and mastering the muscle relaxation techniques explained, will enable you to feel physically more at ease.

- Complete a body audit to identify areas of tension as soon as you have your breathing under control.
- Target the area of discomfort by tensing that muscle group to the count of four.
- Release the tension immediately and enjoy the relaxed state, to the count of four.
- Repeat the above four times for each tense area.

Train your mind and body to relax and this investment will yield a lifetime of dividends.

CHAPTER 16

REHEARSE A POSITIVE SCENE

Use your imagination constructively – what
you think about, you bring about.

The final 'R' in your psychological toolbox is *rehearse*,
as in rehearse a positive scene. Once the body has
been restored to its normal long-term survival mode
by putting the first three 'R's (*react*, *regulate* and
relax) into action, it is essential that you do not allow your
negative thoughts to spiral out of control again, thus creating
another state of acute anxiety/panic. This would only serve
to return you to short-term emergency survival mode and the
preceding sequence would have to be repeated. It is therefore
vital to focus on a positive image or scene that you can call
up at any time to prevent those negative thoughts and feelings from taking hold once more.

The mind and the body are inextricably bound and continuously influence each other. By using the first three 'R's to
stop the fight-or-flight survival response triggered by the
General (amygdala), your body returns to long-term survival
mode and the Sovereign (the neocortex or thinking part of
the brain), which is responsible for making conscious,
rational decisions rather than snap judgements, is back in
power. We need to capitalise on this by immediately exercising this power by taking the initiative with regard to our
choice of thoughts. You do not want the phobia to reassert

itself. This would result in the seat of power switching straight back to the General and the body returning to short-term emergency survival mode, resulting in more stress hormones being released.

The Brain is a Reality Synthesiser

Think how efficiently you are able to induce a state of terror simply by imagining how you might react at the airport. Well, now you are going to turn the tables on the imp (your fear of flying phobia) by picturing yourself in a benign, happy situation. There is a range of techniques that enable us to retain control, and the use of 'positive imagery' is one of them. If we see our brain as a 'reality synthesiser' we can induce a state of calm relaxation by programming our imagination to focus on a topic that is positive and upbeat. John Milton neatly described this phenomenon in his book *Paradise Lost* when he stated that:

> *The mind is its own place, and in itself. Can make a Heav'n of Hell, a Hell of Heav'n.*
>
> *Paradise Lost,* John Milton

In the same way that you can lose yourself in films and feel frightened by a perilous mountain rescue sequence or overjoyed by the hero and heroine being reunited, you can control your mind by selecting the input of your thoughts. As in your reaction to watching the film, your imaginings are not real but virtual. This still produces the same effect since the brain operates on expectations. While watching a daring mountain rescue sequence, you are not in any real danger but your body will react with fear and suspense as though you were there. Research has shown that people can be vicariously traumatised by witnessing distressing events on TV. This is because the locked trance state of the brain has not distinguished between reality and virtual reality.

The good news is that this quality of the brain can be used constructively and the latest neuroscience has shown how this method can also be used to induce pain reduction. By intentionally withdrawing attention from a negative stimulus, such as a dentist's drill or a surgeon's knife, and inducing a trance state by focusing upon a positive image or memory, a patient can experience an operation without anaesthetics.

Just as a patient can reduce physical pain by choosing to concentrate on something positive, so too can psychological distress, such as that experienced by nervous flyers when they step on to an aircraft, be eliminated by focusing on positive thoughts. Remember, though, that this technique can only be employed once the Sovereign (neocortex) is back in control since, as stated in previous chapters, when the General (amygdala) is in charge his emotions/feelings are powerful and override the Sovereign's thoughts.

Positive imagery

This technique involves repeatedly practising or committing to memory a positive scenario, which you can then recall at will. It is effectively the same process as revision, which you will be familiar with from school days. In the same way that you revised thoroughly for tests and exams, learning the information so it would be readily available when needed, we employ the same method for positive visualisation.

The key point to this technique is that you ensure that you keep your brain very busy, performing a positive task, leaving no spare capacity for negativity to creep in and take over. This puts me in mind of the old English proverb that 'an idle mind is the devil's workshop'; however, I would change the word 'devil' for 'imp'. One of the features of people who suffer from phobias is that they tend to have very active imaginations, so the following exercise should not be difficult for you.

The aim is to try to involve all of your senses in perceiving positive imagery to create as detailed and vibrant a scene as you possibly can. The senses of sight and hearing are usually very easy to access, followed by our sense of touch. The final senses of taste and smell are much more difficult to capture; however, these two are worth the extra effort. Smell in particular is wonderfully evocative and can swiftly return us to memories of previous happy experiences.

Convert your fear to hope

Remember that the fear is not real but is a result of your distorted and irrational perception. By proactively harnessing all of your methods of perception, you can constructively use your brain to create a happy, positive outcome.

False	Evidence	Appearing	Real
Have	Only	Positive	Expectations

There is an amazing world out there waiting to be discovered by you – never limit your own horizons.

What follows are a couple of visualisation exercises you can use to help create strong positive imagery with no room for negativity.

SIMPLE VISUALISATION EXERCISE I

Imagine you are lying in a hammock on a tropical beach and try to summon up the following sights, sounds, sensations, smells and taste. As always, make sure that you are breathing correctly to make the experience more powerful and relaxing.

1. Picture a beautiful, sandy beach and azure-blue sea with birds hovering overhead in a perfect, cloudless sky. Can you make out a flotilla of small boats drifting in slow procession along the distant horizon?
2. Now bring your attention to the variety of noises as the waves slowly and majestically roll on to the shore and then trickle back in tiny rivulets to rejoin the ocean. Can you hear the laughter and chatter of small children playing happily in the sand?
3. Allow your arm to dangle outside of the hammock and scoop up a handful of the golden sand, which has been baked by the late afternoon sun. Can you feel the grittiness and warmth of the sand as it trickles between your fingers?
4. Feel the sensation of the gentle breeze as it soothingly cools your warm sun-kissed skin and be aware of your sense of peacefulness and well-being. Can you conjure up the smell of the sun tan lotion that you have applied to your body?
5. Finally, as you lie there enjoying the restful ambience, I invite you to indulge in an ice cream of your choice. Can you taste the deliciously flavoured ice cream as it slips down your throat?

SIMPLE VISUALISATION EXERCISE 2

The following is an example of a description of a peaceful scene, which will enable you to induce a state of relaxation, as long as you first focus on your breathing, making sure that it is slow and measured, before reading through.

I would like you to read the text and try to incorporate all of your senses. It is best to read it in short passages and then close your eyes and focus on trying to summon up as graphically as possible the described image before moving on to the next passage. It doesn't matter how long it takes for you to capture each sense and, furthermore, it doesn't matter if you are not able to capture all of the senses, as it is the process of occupying your brain that is the key to this exercise.

It is even more effective if someone reads this out to you slowly as you listen with closed eyes. Remember that your task is to put your brain through its paces so that it is so busy that no intervening negative thoughts can intrude.

POSITIVE SCENARIO

- At long last it is the weekend. You have had a busy but successful week at work and have managed to complete all the tasks that you had set yourself. So with a light heart, you arrive at your destination in the Lake District, for a glorious weekend of being pampered and cosseted.
- The hotel is wonderfully luxurious with every creature comfort at your disposal. Notice the plumped-up feather pillows and duvet waiting invitingly on your spacious four-poster bed.
- Feel the deep pile rug under your bare feet as you take off your shoes and socks.
- Enjoy your leisurely soak in a fantasia of bubbles and essential oils as you relax in the revitalising warmth of a deep bath.

- Experience the touch of the solid mahogany armrests of your reclining chair as your fingers absently caress its aged contours.
- As the sun begins to sink behind the trees, enjoy its lingering warmth as you sip your pre-dinner drink on the verandah.
- The air is fragrant with the sweet smell of jasmine and you can hear the faint rustle in the branches as birds begin settling down for the night.
- Enjoy the sensation as the cool, thirst-quenching drink slips down your throat and you feel your muscles gently relax while your mind slowly unwinds.
- Feel the pleasant sense of anticipation as you look forward to a succulent gourmet dinner, pleasant company with friends and a well-deserved rest.
- Notice now how slowly and deeply you are breathing as you stretch out languorously on your reclining chair with the dappled reflection of the sun peeping through the trees, dancing on your closed eyelids. Relish this moment of deep inner peace.

Were you able to visualise yourself in the scene described above? Did you manage to engage all, or most, of your senses to experience the sights, sounds, sensations, smells and tastes of the described scene? By focusing on this wonderfully idyllic scene and visualising yourself in this scenario, your mind and body can totally relax and feel instantly calm.

Designing your own scenario

With practice you can efficiently conjure up your own positive setting at will. It doesn't matter what you choose to focus on, as long as it relates to a positive pattern (memory) in your brain. By conjuring up this positive scene, the template will activate the accompanying emotions that were logged at the time of the scene. This is what happens when you look at photographs of various celebrations of long ago. Before you know it you are smiling and re-experiencing the joyous feelings, which accompanied that occasion. Equally, the playing of a song from our past can catapult us straight back to our youth and reawaken all manner of buried memories and emotions.

When preparing your own scenario, I strongly recommend that you give some thought to the following questions:

1. Where do I feel most relaxed, contented or alive?
2. Who is with me?
3. What can I see, hear, touch, smell and taste?
4. What am I doing?

You should try to colour in the scene as much as possible. The more details that you can add, the more vivid and distracting the scenario becomes. Do not feel that your positive scenario has to be passive. Many of my clients feel at their most relaxed and contented while swimming, skiing, entertaining friends and the like. They often describe this feeling as 'being in the zone', totally confident in their skills, be it sailing, dancing, painting or singing. Only you can know which activity creates this sense of contentment and confidence. You may be alone or with friends. You could be looking at a seascape, landscape, cityscape or the familiar furniture and paintings of your home.

As you will now understand, by *you* choosing the agenda instead of allowing your imp (your phobia) to have free rein to induce a state of anticipatory anxiety, you will be able to retrain your brain to stay calm throughout the flight. This exercise can be practised frequently before you fly and will ensure that you have put down a positive template in your brain, thus enabling your 'Sovereign' (neocortex) to stay in control and your 'General' (amygdala) to take a holiday.

Case history

Gus and Edwina, a delightful elderly couple, had never trav-elled much beyond their village in Wales, let alone taken a flight. Both of them were highly suspicious of how a big heavy aircraft could be relied upon to stay up in the sky. Edwina also suffered from claustrophobia and this further fuelled the couple's reluctance to fly. Their son, Billy, a successful lawyer in the City, had organised the Flying with Confidence course for his parents to try to allay some of their insecurities. He believed that they would benefit from voicing their concerns and gaining information and support, which would make them less hesitant about the prospect of flying. Billy's daughter, Stephanie, was getting married later that year and had chosen to have her wedding at her family's holiday home on a Greek island. Stephanie was most emphatic that she wanted her paternal grandparents to be present at the wedding. Gus's health was a little frail and his doctor did not recommend a long arduous journey over land so the family decided to try one more time to persuade the couple to fly. It was also Gus and Edwina's emerald wedding anniversary in six months' time and the extended family wanted to celebrate the occasion by organising a family reunion in the States where Billy's two siblings now lived with their respective families.

Gus and Edwina thoroughly enjoyed the course and gained a little fan club as other participants thought that they were a plucky pair to try something new when they were both not far off their eighties. Before boarding the aircraft, Edwina became a little distressed at the prospect of being in a confined space and started to hyperventilate. With encouragement from her husband she immediately put her new learning into practice and managed to stabilise her breathing. Once on board, Edwina was pleasantly surprised by the spaciousness of the jet's interior and happily settled down in her seat. I asked them during the flight what they thought of the experience. Both of them acknowledged that they loved being able to see so much out of the window but it wasn't really very different from sitting on a bus! There was no doubt that if Gus and Edwina did not make it to the wedding, it would not be down to their inability to fly.

In summary

The final 'R' – *rehearse* – is a very important psychological tool to have at your disposal. You can harness your imagination to create a positive template to carry with you every time you fly. By totally immersing yourself in an imagined positive scene, there is no room for any negative thoughts and feelings to creep in.

- Having relaxed all tense muscle groups, revisit your breathing to ensure that it is still slow and deep.
- Focus on a positive scenario to enable you to remain calm and relaxed. If preferred, close your eyes to facilitate this process.
- Try to endow this positive scenario with as much detail as possible by incorporating all five senses within the depiction.

Capitalise on your relaxed state by choosing a positive scenario from your memory rather than allowing your phobia to make the selection for you.

CHAPTER 17

FULL GUIDED RELAXATION

This chapter pulls together the tools you have learnt so far into a guided visualisation exercise. It incorporates the application of the second, third and fourth 'R's from your toolbox (*regulate*, *relax* and *rehearse*): 'regulating' your breathing, while 'relaxing' various muscle groups, followed by 'rehearsing' visualising a trip to the airport with a flight.

This exercise will enable you to put down a positive template in your brain to help you to deal with your anxiety. Remember how your 'General' (amygdala) pattern matches incoming stimuli to existing data. This guided visualisation will provide a memory trace, which will programme your brain with a positive expectation with regard to your ability to fly. You now have the tools to cope, with any form of anxiety that you may encounter, simply by employing the four 'R's (*react, regulate, relax and rehearse*).

This exercise is in two distinct parts. The first part can be used to calm yourself down in any situation in which you feel anxious. This is achieved by regulating your breathing and learning to relax various muscles. This will enable you to induce a state of relaxation in the mind and body. The second part of the exercise is specifically for those who experience difficulty with flying and will involve a virtual trip to the airport and a flight. If possible, get someone to read the following out loud to you or, alternatively, make a recording, which you can listen to at your convenience.

Part One

The first part consists of doing a guided relaxation exercise to help you to control your stress levels.

Before we start, I would like you to revise the importance of breathing correctly (see Chapter 14, page 150). If at any time throughout the relaxation exercise you experience anxiety, it is essential that you immediately deal with it by regulating your breathing.

If you recall, breathing slowly and deeply is the single most important thing that you can do to ensure that your body does not go into panic mode. Always remember that it is biologically impossible for the body to be in a state of agitation while simultaneously being in a state of relaxation. By slowing down your breathing rate, your body will have no other choice than to relax.

Imagine your speed of breathing regulates a tap. This tap turns on and off the flow of stress hormones such as adrenalin. Rapid, shallow, thoracic breathing turns the tap on and slow, deep diaphragmatic breathing turns the tap off.

Remember that it is the release of the fight-or-flight stress hormones that causes the uncomfortable physical sensations in your body as well as denying you access to the thinking part of the brain. The latter is an essential aspect of the short-term emergency survival mode (see Chapter 11, page 118).

It is therefore imperative that you keep the stress hormones tap turned off. By regulating your breathing, you can return your body to its natural mode of long-term survival if no real threat exists.

Let's begin

Ensure that you are sitting or lying in a comfortable position, with your body well supported. If you are sitting down, make sure that your legs and arms are not crossed. Try to sit as squarely as possible with your back well supported in the chair.

Now, having found a comfortable position, start to focus on your breathing. At the very least, you are aiming to achieve your normal breathing pace. It is better still if you can breathe slower than your usual pace, as this will induce a state of relaxation more rapidly.

Always keep in mind that you are trying to achieve deep, diaphragmatic breathing in which you employ both your chest and abdomen. This ensures that your breathing does not speed up, causing you to hyperventilate. Hyperventilation is recognised by the brain as an organism being in distress. The assumption is that the threat is more serious and this leads to the brain signalling for even more stress hormones to be released into the blood. The ensuing consequences, which if not dissipated through fight or flight, are responsible for your acute discomfort. It is therefore essential that you break this circular reaction, which is maintained by your rapid breathing.

So, to the count of four, breathe in slowly and deeply and say the word *calm* silently to yourself. Then as you breathe out slowly and gently to the count of four, say the word *relax* silently to yourself. Try not to give these words any meaning.

Breathe in two, three, four and out two, three, four. In two, three, four and out two, three, four.

As you breathe in, your stomach should be pushed out, like a balloon being inflated. As you breathe out, your stomach should become flatter as the air is expelled through your mouth, just like a balloon becoming deflated.

So, breathe in two, three, four and out two, three, four. In two, three, four and out two, three, four.

Try to maintain this slow, gentle rhythm throughout the relaxation exercise. Do not be perturbed if at any time you experience a wave of anxiety during the exercise. Just focus fully on your breathing and you will be able to handle the anxiety and return your body to its relaxed state.

Remember that you are totally safe and are doing this guided visualisation exercise as a way of rehearsing for success. Your brain is like a reality synthesiser. Just as you revise for an exam to ensure that you can pass it, similarly you are programming your brain to enable you to fly successfully. If you recall, the brain does not distinguish between reality and virtual reality, so allow yourself to experience this success in the safety of this relaxation exercise.

Now, I would like you to become aware of the background noises in your environment. Depending on where you are conducting this exercise, you may be hearing the hum of air conditioning, the sound of voices, distant traffic, or birds singing outside your window. Whatever the distractions, I would like you to ignore them and only concentrate on these instructions.

As you progress through the relaxation exercise, I would like you to notice the subtle changes in your body as you begin to relax.

You are now going to relax all the muscles in your body, starting from the top of your head to the tips of your toes (see Chapter 15, page 165). At the same time as you relax each muscle group, you will also allow all your cares and worries to go.

So, with your eyes gently closed, start to concentrate on how heavy and sleepy they feel. Let any tension disappear as you allow all the tiny muscles around your eyes to relax. Notice now how smooth and relaxed your temples and eyebrows have become as you allow all the tension to drain away from these areas.

Next, become aware of your facial muscles softening as your cheeks become smooth and your frown vanishes.

Now, focus on your jaw. This is a crucial area in which tension tends to gather, causing discomfort. Allow your upper and lower teeth to part slightly. This will enable your jaw to relax and release any residual tension held in this area.

As you relax these various muscles, remember to check on your breathing from time to time to ensure that you are breathing correctly and maintaining a slow, measured pace. Say the word *calm* as you inhale and *relax* as you exhale, silently to yourself.

So breathe in two, three, four and out two, three, four. In two, three, four and out two, three, four.

As you feel all the tension drain from your head, you begin to drift into a state of deeper and deeper relaxation.

Allow your worries to evaporate as you gently drift into this state of profound relaxation. Enjoy this pleasant sensation as your mind slowly unwinds. You are feeling comfortable, warm and relaxed.

Now think about the muscles in your neck. Allow this warm wave of relaxation to permeate all the muscles in your neck enabling your neck to feel comfortable and relaxed.

Your neck is now feeling warm, comfortable and heavy.

Feel the waves of relaxation pass from your neck into your shoulders and enjoy this warm, heavy sensation.

The feeling of relaxation passes down through your shoulders right through your arms reaching down to the tips of your fingers.

Perhaps you notice a warm, tingling feeling in your fingers or numbness; this is quite normal.

Your arms are now feeling tired and heavy as you sink into a deeper and deeper state of relaxation.

Next, bring your attention to the upper part of the body. If you are sitting, become aware of the sensation of your back and seat against the chair.

Allow this deep wave of relaxation to travel down your spine as you breathe slowly and rhythmically.

Breathe in two, three, four and out two, three, four. In two, three, four and out two, three, four.

As you breathe in, say the word *calm* and as you breathe out, say the word *relax* and allow your body to float into a deeper and deeper state of relaxation.

I would like you to notice how relaxed your chest muscles have become as a consequence of your deep diaphragmatic breathing.

Now allow your stomach to relax. Focus on the gentle rise and fall of your stomach muscles as you slowly breathe in and out. And so these muscles become deeply relaxed.

Enjoy the comfortable sensation as this feeling of deep, heavy relaxation pervades your upper body enabling you to become deeply, deeply relaxed and calm.

Once again, check on your breathing to ensure that you are maintaining a slow gently rhythmical pace. Continue this circular breathing motion by:

Breathing in two, three, four and out two, three, four. In two, three, four and out two, three, four.

Remember to say the word *relax* as you exhale.

Now this warm, comfortable, relaxed feeling flows into your legs as you notice how heavy your limbs have become. The warm, heavy feeling reaches the tips of your toes and you feel all tension drain away from your body.

If you are sitting, become aware of the heaviness of your feet against the floor and imagine all your worries and cares leaving your body and being absorbed by the floor below.

If you are lying down, experience the heaviness of your entire body, as your cares and worries are absorbed by the surface supporting you.

Your mind is becoming totally still and deeply, deeply relaxed. Concentrate on how your whole body feels as you enjoy this deliciously deep state of profound relaxation. Your body is floating and drifting, feeling warm, comfortable and heavy. So heavy that it seems impossible to raise your limbs even if you wanted to.

Your mind is also enjoying this comfortable sleepy sensation as you sink into a deeper and deeper state of profound relaxation.

Once again, focus on your breathing for a few moments and notice now how slowly and deeply you are breathing in and out, saying the words *calm* and *relax* as you inhale and exhale. Enjoy these sensations for a few moments, and allow your body and mind to become empty as you drift into a deeper and deeper state of profound relaxation.

Part Two

Now that you are totally, deeply relaxed and still enjoying the warm, heavy feeling throughout your body, I want you to be aware that you are going on a journey. Do not be concerned if you experience feelings of anxiety from time to time; this is quite normal. You now have the tools to deal with these feelings.

Remember to focus on your breathing. Take a deep breath and as you inhale say the word *calm* and as you exhale say to yourself *relax*. You will then replace the feelings of anxiety with a sense of calmness.

Remember that you are in control and can return your body to a state of relaxation simply by regulating your breathing.

Each time you experience tension just bring back these warm, heavy feelings of relaxation by:

Breathing in two, three, four and out two, three, four. In two, three, four and out two, three, four.

Remember that today is different. You are doing things differently. You can take back control at any time.

We are rehearsing this journey for success. Allow yourself to experience this positive outcome. So in a state of calmness you make your way to the airport. See yourself arriving at the airport.

Notice the bright lights and be aware of all the bustle and activity going on around you.

You hear the announcements on the public address system, and are aware of the other passengers and airport officials.

You make your way to the check-in desk, remembering that you are in control.

You calmly and confidently go through the various security checks, passport control and arrive in the departure lounge. Calmly, you take a seat, and take this opportunity to focus on your breathing and relaxing your muscles. You breathe in slowly and deeply to the count of four saying the word *calm* as you inhale and *relax* as you exhale.

Breathing in two, three, four and out two, three, four. In two, three, four and out two, three, four.

You sit there waiting for your flight to be called, knowing that if you do become anxious, you can now handle the situation. Focus on your breathing and allow those warm, heavy, relaxed feelings to return. Your flight has been called, and you go confidently through the departure gate, and calmly make your way to the aircraft.

As you board the aircraft, you are greeted by the friendly smiles of the flight attendants.

You calmly present your boarding pass, and are directed towards your seat.

As you go down the aisle to your seat, you notice the other passengers stowing away their bags and coats, and settling down in their seats. You are confident and in control as you locate your seat, fasten your belt and absorb your surroundings.

You hear the activity around you as overhead lockers are closed and seatbelts are fastened, in preparation for take-off. Take this opportunity to focus on your breathing once more, and enjoy those warm, heavy feelings as you relax in your seat.

Now you hear the captain asking the cabin crew to prepare the doors for take-off.

You may be given further information about your flight, such as the altitude at which the aeroplane will fly, expected weather conditions, and estimated arrival time.

You notice that the engines have been started up. The aeroplane begins to taxi towards the runway from which it will depart. Once clearance has been received from Air Traffic Control, the aircraft begins to move down the runway gathering speed.

You may wish to look out of the window or concentrate once more on your breathing.

Remember to breathe slowly and deeply, saying the words *calm* as you inhale and *relax* as you exhale.

So, in two, three, four and out two, three, four. In two, three, four and out two, three, four.

Suddenly the rattling and shaking stops as the aeroplane gently takes off from the runway.

The aircraft steadily climbs, as you relax back into your seat during the ascent. If you experience anxiety at any point, you take control, by focusing once again on your breathing and relaxing. You breathe slowly and deeply, saying the words *calm* as you inhale and *relax* as you exhale.

So, in two, three, four and out two, three, four. In two, three, four and out two, three, four.

You will hear a variety of different noises as the landing gear is retracted, the noise abatement procedure is put into action, and the aircraft adjusts to its cruising altitude.

These are all good noises, which you now understand, and they no longer cause you anxiety.

Once the aeroplane has levelled off, the pilot switches off the seatbelt sign, and the cabin crew begin to move around. You may decide to read a book, chat to your neighbour, look out of the window or just sit back and relax.

If you look out of the window, you will see the land below, or maybe cloud formations. If it is night-time, you will see the bright lights below becoming more and more distant as the aeroplane steadily ascends.

You check your breathing from time to time, making sure that it is slow and deep, enabling you to feel confident and relaxed throughout the flight.

If at any time the aircraft goes through turbulence, you recall that turbulence may be experienced as uncomfortable but it is never ever dangerous. You repeat the mantra that it is never ever dangerous.

You know that you can cope with this experience by focusing on your breathing. You notice that people are moving around the aircraft, chatting to each other and the crew. You might decide to stretch your legs and take a little walk too.

Depending on the length of the flight, there may be a drinks service followed by a meal. After your meal you may decide to watch a film, read a book or magazine or take a nap to enable you to arrive at your destination feeling refreshed and relaxed.

Before you know it, the captain is informing you that the descent has started and you refasten your seatbelt in readiness for landing.

Once again, you will experience the various noises in reverse, as the landing gear is lowered. You now understand these noises and they no longer cause you any anxiety.

The engine rhythm changes, as the aircraft gradually descends and reduces to landing speed. You are confident that you are in control, as you breathe in deeply, and out slowly, saying the words *calm* as you inhale and *relax* as you exhale.

Any anxiety you might experience is dealt with by simply regulating your breathing.

The wheels touch down, and the aircraft decelerates along the runway.

You are smiling and happy as you acknowledge your excellent achievement. You have confronted your fear and now feel strong and confident. You have done things differently and have coped with your anxiety.

You have taken another step towards taking back real control of your life. You are back in charge and have tamed or evicted the imp (phobia) that had stolen so many aspects of your life.

You now can choose where you wish to travel to for a holiday. You can decide whether to accept the promotion that involves travel because now you know that travel is no longer an obstacle to your career opportunities.

The aircraft comes to a complete stop, the seatbelt signs are switched off, and you are invited to disembark. You are happy, confident and smiling, as you make your way through the airport.

Think about what you are now able to do. Picture yourself feeling this new level of control. Take a few moments to relish this wonderful sense of achievement.

Now, I would like you to slowly bring your attention back to the room you are in. Become aware of the chair you are sitting on or the bed on which you are lying. Start to notice the noises around you.

When you are ready, slowly open your eyes.

Remember that this is your life and you have a right to make choices unencumbered by imps (phobias) that try to steal your options.

You are now equipped with the tools to live your life rather than exist in it as a mere pawn of the phobia. The art of liberation from anxiety lies quite simply in your ability to regulate your breathing. So learn to manage your lungs and take back control of your life.

There is a most wonderful world out there for you to discover and I wish you many happy holidays to come, now that you know how to fly with confidence.

Twenty years from now you will be more disappointed by the things you didn't do than by the ones you did do. So throw off the bowlines, sail away from the safe harbour. Catch the trade winds in your sails. Explore. Dream. Discover.

Mark Twain

CHAPTER 18

A REMINDER OF THE FOUR 'R'S

How to React

- As soon as you feel anxious place a rubber band on your wrist and twang it sufficiently so that it hurts!
- Say to yourself '*stop*' either silently or out loud if you prefer.
- Follow this up immediately with a positive statement/affirmation like:
  '*I can do this because I am in control and I refuse to allow a bully to dictate my life for me.*'

Regulate Breathing

- Focus on your breathing immediately after twanging the rubber band and expressing a positive affirmation.
- Sit comfortably and exhale the air from your body.
- Inhale to the count of four, saying the word '*calm*' to yourself.
- Exhale to the count of four, saying the word '*relax*' to yourself.
- Repeat the previous two steps until your breathing is brought under control.

Relax Muscles

- As soon as you have your breathing under control, complete a body audit to identify areas of tension.

- Target the area of discomfort by tensing that muscle group to the count of four.
- Release the tension immediately and enjoy the relaxed state to the count of four.
- Repeat the above four times for each tense area.

Fourth 'R' – Rehearse a Positive Scene

- Having relaxed all tense muscle groups, revisit your breathing to ensure that it is still slow and deep.
- Focus on a positive scenario to enable you to remain calm and relaxed. If preferred, close your eyes to facilitate this process.
- Try to endow this positive scenario with as much detail as possible by incorporating all five senses within the depiction.

Useful points to keep in mind

1. Try to not take yourself or life too seriously as this promotes stress.
2. Learn to be flexible and less rigid as this reduces stress.
3. Adopt a positive attitude to life. This conserves energy rather than wasting it on needless and useless worrying.
4. Make the incorporation of relaxation techniques, quality sleep, exercise and healthy eating part of your daily routine.
5. Learn to breathe correctly as this is the single most important way that you can induce a state of relaxation.
6. Avoid black-and-white thinking, since most things in life are not either, nor are most situations.
7. Don't indulge in 'what if?' scenarios as citing endless implausible possibilities is a waste of energy and is totally self-defeating.

8. Stop irrational probability bias as in 'I am never going to win the lottery' and 'I will definitely be in an accident'.

9. Inform the crew that you are an anxious flyer as this will enable them to offer you the reassurance you need throughout the flight.

10. If you suffer from claustrophobia, try to close your eyes and imagine that you are at home sitting in your favourite comfortable chair.

11. When flying, do not wear tight garments as most people swell up a little when on an aircraft due to the constant sitting and inactivity. The discomfort of feeling cut in half by wearing too tight a waistband will increase your stress levels.

12. Try to avoid drinking too much alcohol on a flight since the impact of the higher altitude makes its effect more rapid and intoxicating.

13. Dehydration is more likely on a flight due to the reduced moisture in the cabin; therefore it is important to drink lots of water while on board.

14. Try to avoid taking acidic foods like meat and cheese to excess.

15. Some people find that Bach Rescue Remedy and flower remedies such as Mimulus are useful to help keep them calm. Aromatherapy oils such as clary sage, lavender or valerian can also be used to help you to relax by putting a few drops on a handkerchief before and/or during the flight.

16. Limit the consumption of stimulants such as coffee, tea (apart from herbal teas like camomile – which is good for both you and Peter Rabbit!) colas and chocolate. But also remember that a little of what you fancy does you good!

CHAPTER 19

CONCLUSION

We hope that by reading this book you are now armed with all the knowledge you need to enable you to debunk many of the false beliefs you have previously entertained, which would have played a significant part in preventing you from flying with confidence.

You should now understand the importance of facing your phobia head on rather than languishing in denial by pretending that you can get by perfectly well in life not being able to fly. As we have said previously, 'getting by' is not a preferred option when life is for living. Whether you want to go to a family member's wedding or enjoy the beautiful scenery of a faraway place such as New Zealand, once you overcome your fear of flying the whole world is open to you.

After reading this book, some of you will go on your next flight, apply your new-found knowledge and completely conquer your phobia. For others, change will be more gradual and you will need to apply the tools you have learnt on several flights before being able to fly with confidence. Remember that we are all unique and as a consequence we each achieve change at different speeds. Never compare yourself to anyone else, as it is unrealistic to imagine that we all have identical difficulties in the first place or the same resources to deal with them.

Whichever type of person you are, the key to overcoming your fear is be proactive, have self-belief, instil a positive attitude, and apply your new knowledge and tools. Now you can go out and discover the world. All that remains is for us to wish our readers many happy 'Bon Voyages' and we hope that one day you will enjoy flying just as much as we do.

The Three Golden Principles

1. Trust the airline industry. They operate a zero tolerance policy towards anything that compromises your safety, making flying undeniably the safest form of travel.
2. Exercise real control over your life by always challenging irrational fears. Avoidance exacerbates the problem and confrontation solves the problem.
3. Remember that it is biologically impossible to be in a state of agitation while simultaneously being in a state of relaxation. To avoid a panic attack learn to induce the relaxation mode by implementing the four 'R's.

Don't allow the insidious proliferation of fear and anxiety to consume your life. Make a stand today and reclaim the person you were born to be, not a creature of fear trembling in the shadows but a true adventurer embracing the richness of life along with all the wonderful experiences it affords.

FURTHER HELP

Addiction NI
Tel: 02890 664434
Email: enquiries@addictionni.com

Alcoholics Anonymous
Tel: 0845 769 7555
Email: help@alcoholics-anonymous.org.uk

Anxiety UK
Tel: 08444 775 774
Email: info@anxietyuk.org.uk

Beat (Beat Eating Disorders)
Tel: 0845 634 1414 (Adult)
Tel: 0845 634 7650 (Youth)
Email: info@b-eat.co.uk

British Airways Flying with Confidence
Tel: 01252 793250
www.flyingwithconfidence.com

British Association for Behavioural and Cognitive Therapies
Tel: 0161 705 4304
Email: babcp@babcp.com

British Association for Counselling and Psychotherapy
Tel: 01455 883316
Email: bacp@bacp.co.uk

British Psychological Society
Tel: 0116 254 9568
Email: enquiry@bps.org.uk

Depression UK
Email: info@depressionuk.org
www.depressionuk.org/

Drinksense
Tel: 01733 555532
Email: centraloffice@drinksense.org

Eating Disorders Support
Tel: 01494 793223
Email: support@eatingdisorderssupport.co.uk
www.eatingdisorderssupport.co.uk

Flying advice from Dr Keith Stoll
Email: Harley.house@btconnect.com
www.lessonsfrommypatients.com

Guided Relaxation Resources
Email: info@widenmind.com
www.widenmind.com

International Stress Management Association
Tel: 0845 680 7083
Email: stress@isma.org.uk

The Mental Health Foundation
Tel: 020 7803 1100
Email: mhf@mhf.org.uk

Mind
Tel: 0300 123 3393
Email: info@mind.org.uk

National Centre for Eating Disorders
Tel: 0845 838 2040
Email: admin@ncfed.com

National Counselling Society
Tel: 0870 850 3389
www.nationalcounsellingsociety.org

No Panic
Tel: 0808 808 0545
Email: ceo@nopanic.org.uk

OCD Action
Tel: 0845 390 6232
Email: support@ocdaction.org.uk

Patricia Furness-Smith
Tel: 01494 766 246
www.maturus.co.uk

Relate (relationship support and counselling)
Tel: 0300 100 1234
www.relate.org.uk

The Sleep Council
Tel: 0800 018 7923
Email: info@sleepcouncil.com

UK Psychological Trauma Society
Email: UKPTSinfo@googlemail.com
www.ukpts.co.uk

ACKNOWLEDGEMENTS

We would like to thank a number of people who have helped in the creation of this book. So, as they say on reality TV, 'in no particular order', we would like to express our deepest gratitude to our respective much-loved and long-suffering families. This includes our parents, children, spouses – and Faustus – who have provided encouragement, criticism, constructive and otherwise, wine and licks in that order.

We thank all of our wonderful course participants and clients as it is through their openness and trust that we have learned so much from their experience. Thank you to British Airways for all the brilliant support which they have given to the Flying with Confidence courses. Steve would like to express his gratitude to James Hicks, friend and cadet pilot, for providing the latest training information, Tony Allright and Tony Brown, for proofreading the technical section, and Dr Helen Corlett, for her advice within the technical section. Also, Peter Hughes, Steve's business partner, for introducing him to Aviatours. Following in the same vein, Patricia would like to thank Steve's wife, Donna, friend and ex-student, for introducing her to Aviatours.

Huge thanks go to Louise Francis, our editor, who not only invited Patricia to write this book but also offered timely guidance at every juncture. Louise, your positive, gentle and patient approach made it possible for two very busy people to find the time to sit down and write this book, albeit in stolen snatches. Patricia would also like to acknowledge the invaluable input from her father-in-law, Gerald Furness-Smith, who kindly read through the psychological section. Being a lawyer, this was not his usual métier and thus he was able to comment, with pertinence and causticity, on anything that remotely verged on psychobabble! I am indebted to him for his layman's perspective, which has helped me to keep my feet firmly on the ground!

Naturally, we are both extremely grateful to our publisher, Vermilion, Ebury Publishing, for giving us this opportunity. Finally, our thanks go to our illustrator, Stephen Dew, and book cover designer, Toby Clarke, for their much-appreciated creative talents.

INDEX